For more than a quarter century, Senator Jesse Helms of North Carolina has been a leading voice in America's most important foreign policy debates. Lady Margaret Thatcher puts it succinctly in her foreword to this volume: "Senator Jesse Helms's record as a freedom fighter is unmatched."

In *Empire for Liberty*, Senator Helms articulates his clear, principled approach to U.S. foreign policy: "I believe in a sovereign America. I believe she has a moral mission: to fan the flames of freedom across the globe. But I am convinced that the only way America can fulfill that moral mission, and become the 'Empire for Liberty' Jefferson hoped we would be, is to defend and protect our liberties, our Constitution, and our national sovereignty."

Senator Helms in these essays and speeches focuses on the emerging threats to America's sovereignty as well as our obligations to defend freedom around the world. In tackling today's most important and controversial foreign policy issues—from the threat posed by Communist China, to nuclear proliferation and missile

Empire for Liberty

Empire for Liberty

A Sovereign America and Her Moral Mission

Jesse Helms

Foreword by
Margaret Thatcher

Edited by
Marc Thiessen

Library of Congress Cataloging-in-Publication Data

Helms, Jesse.
    Empire for liberty : a sovereign America and her moral mission / introduction by Margaret Thatcher.
        p. cm.
    ISBN 0-89526-168-5 (alk. paper)
    1. United States—Foreign relations—1993– 2. Helms, Jesse—Political and social views. I. Title.

E838.5 .H432 2001
327.73—dc21

                                                                        2001019397

Published in the United States by
Regnery Publishing, Inc.
An Eagle Publishing Company
One Massachusetts Avenue, NW
Washington, DC 20001

Visit us at www.regnery.com

Distributed to the trade by
National Book Network
4720-A Boston Way
Lanham, MD 20706

Printed on acid-free paper
Manufactured in the United States of America

10 9 8 7 6 5 4 3 2 1

Books are available in quantity for promotional or premium use. Write to Director of Special Sales, Regnery Publishing, Inc., One Massachusetts Avenue, NW, Washington, DC 20001, for information on discounts and terms or call (202) 216-0600.

Permissions are on page 211.

Every good faith effort has been made in this work to credit sources and comply with the fairness doctrine on quotation and use of research material. If any copyrighted material has been inadvertently used in this work without proper credit being given in one manner or another, please the publisher in writing so that future printings of this work may be corrected accordingly.

For Bud Nance

*"We should have such an
Empire for Liberty as [the world]
has never surveyed since the Creation...."*

*Thomas Jefferson, in a letter to
James Madison, April 27, 1809*

Contents

Acknowledgments   xiii
Foreword by Margaret Thatcher   xv
Preface by Jesse Helms   xix

Part I: A Sovereign America...

Chapter 1:   SAYING NO   3
             Sometimes It's Our Job to Say No

Chapter 2:   INTERNATIONAL "JUSTICE"   9
             Slay This Monster
             And after Pinochet?
             Why Israel Must Not Sign the ICC Treaty

Chapter 3:   THE DYSFUNCTIONAL
             UNITED NATIONS   23
             Mr. Boutros-Ghali Has to Change His Tune
             Saving the UN
             A Day to Pay Old Debts
             American Sovereignty and the United Nations
             A Welcome to Washington

Chapter 4:   NATO—AN ALLIANCE THAT WORKS   57
             New Members, Not New Missions
             NATO Expansion Has All the Safeguards
                It Needs

Chapter 5:   THE ARMS CONTROL HERESY   67
             Committing to Missile Defense
             Why the Senate Said No to the Nuclear
                Test Ban Treaty
             Amend the ABM Treaty? No, Scrap It
             Clinton's Toothless Nonproliferation Policy
             A Treaty That's Worse Than Nothing
             The Flaws in the Chemical Weapons Treaty

Part II: ...And Her Moral Mission

Chapter 6:   A MORAL FOREIGN POLICY   91
              What Sanctions Epidemic?

Chapter 7:   CHINA   103
              Two Chinese States
              What Are We Going to Do about China?
              Red China, Free China
              Hong Kong: Exit Britain, Enter America
              Most Favored Nation?

Chapter 8:   THE BOSNIAN FREEDOM FIGHTERS   123
              Apply the Reagan Doctrine in Bosnia
              Let's Help Arm the Bosnians
              Send Arms, Not Troops

Chapter 9:   KOSOVO—GETTING RID
              OF MILOSEVIC   133
              Milosevic Must Go

Chapter 10:   CUBA—CASTRO'S TROPICAL GULAG   137
              Trade with Castro? No Cigar
              Cubans Meet Their Liberator
              Reaching Out to the People of Cuba
              Allies without a Moral Compass
              Tourists Won't Liberate Cuba
              Castro Blows a Gasket
              Why Helms-Burton?

Chapter 11:   THE MIDDLE EAST   159
              Hafez al-Assad, Murderer
              Middle East Blackmail

Chapter 12:   HAITIAN "DEMOCRACY"   165
              Letting Aristide Get Away with Murder

Chapter 13:   THE WAR ON DRUGS   169
              Colombia: America's Favorite
                  Narco-Democracy (*with William J. Bennett*)
              The Challenge to Colombia
              Defeat the Narco-Guerrillas

Chapter 14: A COMPASSIONATE
CONSERVATIVE FOREIGN POLICY 181
Toward a Compassionate Conservative
Foreign Policy
Chapter 15: THE REAGAN REVOLUTION
AND A MORAL FOREIGN POLICY 199
The Lasting Leadership of Ronald Reagan

Permissions 211

Acknowledgments

THIS VOLUME IS DEDICATED to my longtime best friend, Admiral James W. Nance, the late and much loved chief of staff of the Senate Foreign Relations Committee. Bud and I were born two months apart, two blocks apart, in Monroe, North Carolina.

I am thankful for the dedicated labor of the Foreign Relations Committee family that Bud put together. Steve Biegun was Bud's and my choice as successor to Bud as chief of staff. Marc Thiessen edited this volume and wrote the chapter introductions.

I am so grateful to all of the classy young people who have served on the committee staff during my years as chairman: Andrew Anderson, Jacqueline Aronson, Christa Bailey, Sara Battaglia, Lisa Benham, Steve Berry, Lauren Bessent, Marshall Billingslea, Beth Bonargo, Ellen Bork, Thomas Brady, Jamie Brown, Ian Brzezinski, Martha Cagle, Tom Callahan, Christine Clark, Elisabeth De Moss, Jim Doran, Richard Douglas, Dan Fisk, Richard Fontaine, Adam Frey, Sherry Grandjean, Taylor Griffin, Garrett Grigsby, Gina Marie Hatheway, Chuck James, Tom Kleine, Mark Lagon, Elizabeth Lambird, Kirsten Madison, Scott Mclean, Patricia McNerney, Christopher Moore, Christa

Muratore, Colleen Noonan, Roger Noriega, Susan Oursler, Laura Parker, Kristin Peck, Danielle Pletka, Nancy Ray, Kelly Siekman, Anne Smith, Elizabeth Stewart, Christopher Walker, Natasha Watson, Christopher Weld, Michael Westphal, Michael Willner, Hannah Williams, and Susan Williams.

I am thankful, as well, to the greatest British prime minister since Winston Churchill, Margaret Thatcher, not only for agreeing to write the foreword to this volume but also for the wonderful example of leadership she has given Britain, America, and the world.

It would be remiss of me to fail to express my appreciation to the editors of the fine newspapers and journals who were originally publishers of the essays contained herein, including the *Washington Post*, *The Weekly Standard*, the *Wall Street Journal*, the *Miami Herald*, *Izvestia* (if anyone had told me when I got to the Senate twenty-nine years ago I'd be writing for *Izvestia* ...), the *Washington Times*, *USA Today*, *Cigar Aficionado*, the *Los Angeles Times*, Hong Kong's *Apple Daily*, *Ha'aretz*, *Foreign Affairs*, the *New York Times*, the *Financial Times*, and *American Heritage*. Grateful acknowledgment is made to those who provided permission to reprint.

I am especially grateful to the good folks at Regnery for publishing this volume; their hard work and remarkable editorial and design assistance made the difference.

Then there are John Dodd and all the other great people at the Jesse Helms Center in Wingate, North Carolina—I am grateful for their devoted work in making this book possible.

And none of this would have been possible without the caring support of Dorothy Coble Helms, my best friend for nearly fifty-nine years.

Foreword

SENATOR JESSE HELMS'S RECORD as a freedom fighter is unmatched. Throughout the Cold War he maintained an implacable but always acute and articulate hostility to communism. He steadfastly refused to compromise with a system that President Reagan rightly termed an "Evil Empire." And his convictions were triumphantly validated by that empire's ignominious collapse—in circumstances so embarrassing for Senator Helms's critics that they have been rewriting them ever since.

Many right-of-center parties and politicians around the world emerged from that period with their sense of political direction apparently impaired. It was as if they questioned their own relevance once the world around them became a more complex place.

But, as he powerfully demonstrates in these essays, Senator Helms has never suffered from these debilitating doubts. He understands that the continuity between the Cold War and post–Cold War worlds is far greater than many pundits conceive. He is fully aware that the international scene is still replete with dangers, new and old. And he entirely comprehends that only a clear, principled, conservative approach can ensure that America and her allies rise to the challenges that confront us.

In America and elsewhere there has sometimes seemed to be a tendency for conservatives to fall into the traps of isolationism on the one hand or universalism on the other. We have, on occasion, allowed our critics to make us choose between extreme positions of nonintervention and intervention everywhere, which are both equally unrealistic. President Reagan and I did not feel this temptation; nor, quite evidently, does Jesse Helms.

So, for example, Senator Helms is splendidly unembarrassed in entitling his volume *Empire for Liberty* (a phrase borrowed, with attribution, from Thomas Jefferson). The senator has a proud belief in America's mission, which he rightly describes as "moral."

America is, indeed, unlike other countries. This is not just because she is now the only superpower. Rather, it is because America's greatness is based upon beliefs and values to which she has to give global expression if she is to remain true to herself. Senator Helms believes that America and the West had to reverse and punish Serb aggression in Bosnia and Kosovo, and he is convinced that we should not buckle now before China. He is also rightly determined that the West should not give succor to Fidel Castro's odious and oppressive tyranny.

But, of course, none of this "moral" approach to foreign policy makes Mr. Helms an internationalist, in the sense that the new liberal clerisy envisages. So Senator Helms argues that it is vital that America resist attempts to shackle her freedom of maneuver and to impede her (and our) sovereignty through the activity of a new International Criminal Court—perhaps the single silliest idea yet dreamed up by our New Left internationalist masters.

He also condemns the sham justice meted out to former president Pinochet under the cover of concern for "human rights," rightly seeing this shameful affair as revealing the shape of things to come. He has consistently attacked utopian projects of arms control—such as the outmoded ABM Treaty—which inhibit the vital task of national defense, and he has called for the urgent construction of a global ballistic missile defense system.

A conservative foreign policy can be defined in a variety of ways. I suggest, though, that it is essentially one which places the national interest first and which never seeks to employ national resources to create an international utopia. But I would add that it is also one which recognizes that power brings responsibility and (as another well-known dictum has it) that all that is necessary for evil to triumph is that good men do nothing. There will always be a tension between these practical and moral imperatives. But then nobody ever said that international statesmanship was easy. Nor has it been easy for Jesse Helms to speak out so clearly and consistently for American and wider Western interests. I admire him for it.

Margaret Thatcher
London, England
May 2001

Preface

LYING SICK AND NEAR DEATH AT HIS HOME, Monticello, on June 24, 1826, Thomas Jefferson lifted his pen and wrote a brief note to Roger C. Weightman, declining his invitation to come to Washington for the fiftieth anniversary celebration of the Declaration of Independence.

His failing health would not permit him to join the citizens of Washington that day, Jefferson wrote, but he shared with them this wish for the Declaration he had written fifty years before:

> May it be to the world, what I believe it will be (to some parts sooner, to others later, but finally to all): the signal arousing men to burst the chains under which monkish ignorance and superstition had persuaded them to bind themselves, and assume the blessings and security of self-government.... All eyes are opened, or are opening to the rights of man ... [and] the palpable truth that the mass of mankind has not been born with saddles on their backs, nor a favored few booted and spurred, ready to ride them legitimately by the grace of God.

These were the last words from Thomas Jefferson's pen.

These final words to his fellow Americans, expressing the hope that the revolution in human liberty that they had begun should spread to all corners of the earth, came from the same Thomas Jefferson who some years earlier uttered the famous warning to his countrymen against "entangling alliances."

Was Jefferson an "internationalist" or an "isolationist"?

As the title of this book indicates, Jefferson envisioned America becoming what he termed an "Empire for Liberty as [the world] has never surveyed since the Creation." But he was, at the same time, a jealous guardian of America's sovereignty. To him, these were not contradictory positions. If America was to promote freedom abroad, he believed, Americans must be eternally vigilant in protecting their freedoms at home.

Today, some in the so-called "human rights" community are seeking to convince us that the opposite is true—that the way to promote Jeffersonian democracy abroad is to sacrifice American liberty at home. America, they insist, must be willing to cede its sovereignty to a profusion of international institutions (such as the United Nations and the proposed International Criminal Court) and submit its conduct at home and abroad to the judgment of the world, through a plethora of treaties which they claim will ban every conceivable form of abuse and every weapons system known to man.

What they are proposing is not a path to greater liberty but rather a shortcut to tyranny. They would bind America up in a straitjacket formed from these treaties and institutions. And in so doing, they would have us sacrifice our freedom of action to defend not only our own liberty but that of others as well.

I stand with Jefferson and the rest of the Founding Fathers on the principle that if we are to promote liberty abroad, we cannot—must not—sacrifice our liberties at home.

With the defeat of fascism and communism this century, the revolution in human liberty that Jefferson envisioned has indeed spread around the globe. Yes, there are many glaring holdouts, but more and more nations are joining the ranks of the free each year.

This revolution was not made possible by the United Nations. It was not made possible by an International Criminal Court. It was made possible by America—through both her example and her leadership of the free world.

Despite this recent history, the world is fast abandoning the international order that won the Cold War. Multilateralism is becoming the prevailing current in international affairs today. Our European allies (who should know better) are running head-long into the multilateralist camp, ceding more and more of their sovereignty to the European Union, the United Nations, and other emerging supranational institutions. And they are per-plexed, aghast, and appalled that America is refusing to go along.

But America is different.

Americans know full well that in order to conduct a foreign policy guided by the virtues on which our own democracy was founded, as Jefferson hoped, we must be willing to make many sacrifices, in treasure and, in some cases, lives. But there is one thing we Americans must never, ever, sacrifice: our sovereignty.

If we are to continue the expansion of Jefferson's democratic experiment, we must heed his warnings against entangling America in a profusion of treaties and institutions that will serve only to con-strain us from defending our moral and national security interests—and that will be used by jealous nations to attack America and prevent her from fulfilling her moral mission in the world.

It is with these thoughts that the decision was made to offer this collection of essays, written during my tenure as chairman of the Senate Foreign Relations Committee. This collection is subtitled *A Sovereign America and Her Moral Mission*, and the essays contained herein are focused on those two themes. The first section focuses on the emerging threats to America's security and her sovereignty, and how we must confront them; the second section discusses our obligations to defend freedom around the world and build an "empire for liberty."

These essays were written to address the key foreign policy debates of the past six years. They include a wide range of topics— our relations with China and Taiwan, the wars in Bosnia and Kosovo, the battle for freedom in Cuba, the expansion of NATO, and reform of the dysfunctional United Nations, among others. But I believe the reader will find several consistent themes emerging.

First, America should stand with the democrats (note the small "d"!)—be they in China or Serbia, Bosnia or Cuba—even if it means sacrificing opportunities for trade. We cannot, and must not, send American troops to every far-flung corner of the world. But where democrats are willing to stand up to dictators, America should be willing to give them aid—moral, diplomatic, financial, and (where appropriate) military—so long as doing so does not harm America's own vital security interests. We must not hesitate for one second to sanction and ostracize regimes that torture their own people, murder American citizens, or flood our streets with drugs.

Second, when it comes to our national defense, scraps of paper are no substitute for concrete defenses. We must never allow arms control treaties (e.g., the Anti-Ballistic Missile Treaty) to forbid our taking the steps necessary to defend America. The theology of arms control is a heresy that must be rejected.

Third, we must view with extreme caution the plethora of international human rights treaties and emerging human rights "law." International law once governed only relations between states.

Today, a change is emerging in which a new class of unelected international bureaucrats is presuming to sit in judgment of the actions of sovereign states. For our part, the United States should under no circumstances allow the conduct of America's domestic affairs (much less our foreign affairs) to be placed before the judgment of this new class of international political commissars. Treaties and institutions that propose to interfere in how our nation runs its business, denying us the flexibility to defend our national interests, must be rejected.

Where good international institutions exist (and they do), they have usually succeeded because they have resisted the temptation to remake the world and have focused instead on a limited mission. This is clearly the case with the NATO alliance, whose expansion to include Poland, Hungary, and the Czech Republic I strongly supported (and is documented in this volume). But if the Atlantic alliance is to continue to succeed, we must protect it by ensuring it remains true to its core functions and is not saddled by multilateralist utopians with a plethora of new missions which will destroy its very being.

Where dysfunctional institutions—such as the United Nations—exist, we should press them to reform, seek to limit their missions, and prevent them at all costs from assuming any trappings of sovereignty—such as the ability to collect taxes, maintain a standing army, or establish a permanent judiciary—and from usurping ours.

I believe in a sovereign America. I believe she has a moral mission: to fan the flames of freedom across the globe. But I am convinced that the only way America can fulfill that moral mission, and become the "Empire for Liberty" Jefferson hoped we would be, is to defend and protect our liberties, our Constitution, and our national sovereignty.

It is my hope that the reader will find this volume a reflection of these aims, to which I have tried to dedicate my public career, as well as, I hope, an interesting chronicle of the foreign policy battles that have ensued in recent years and of those certain to ensue at the start of this new century.

Jesse Helms
Raleigh, North Carolina
May 2001

Part I
A Sovereign America...

Chapter 1
Saying No

WHEN THE FOUNDING FATHERS established the U.S. Senate, they meant it to be a brake on impulsive instincts. Sometimes the Senate's job is to say no.

As Senator Helms explains in this essay, written for *American Heritage* magazine, he is by no means the first chairman of the Senate Foreign Relations Committee to be vilified by the media for refusing to go along with the wishes of America's foreign policy elite. Indeed, he argues, it is the very role of a Foreign Relations Committee chairman to say no from time to time.

SOMETIMES IT'S OUR JOB TO SAY NO
American Heritage, December 1998

I HAVE OCCASIONALLY BEEN referred to as "Senator No," and I'm proud of the title. But when it comes to saying no, I'm not even in the same ballpark with the first North Carolinian to serve as chairman of the Senate Foreign Relations Committee—Nathaniel Macon.

A Revolutionary War veteran and native of Warrenton, Senator Macon was chairman between 1825 and 1829. He was a fierce opponent of any and all measures to expand the power of

3

the new federal government. Indeed, during his entire tenure in Congress, it was said that Macon cast more no votes than did any ten other members combined.

He believed what I believe: Saying no is a part of the job of being the Foreign Relations Committee chairman. As much as some might wish it otherwise, the committee was never meant to be a rubber stamp for administration policies.

Of course, this fact does not please everyone. Take the following passage from the journal *Foreign Affairs*:

> [The senator] exercises the power of protest and veto.... It would not occur to [him] that he must sacrifice any of his liberty of action because he had become Chairman of the Committee on Foreign Relations. He has always spoken his mind on all subjects, and he continues to speak it. If he does not like French policy... or British policy... he says so loudly and publicly. He feels perfectly free to indulge in running comment on the acts of foreign powers... and on any and all negotiations however delicate at any time while they are in progress.... The ensuing troubles of the Executive do not break his heart.... As a matter of fact, he regards it as his high duty to watch the Executive with the utmost suspicion.... He is...determined...to make the Senate a major partner in diplomatic affairs.

That essay was not written about me (though I would plead nolo contendere if it had been). It was written in January 1926 by Walter Lippmann about Senator William Borah of Idaho, who succeeded Henry Cabot Lodge as chairman in 1924. (While I don't subscribe to all of Senator Borah's views, I sure do like his style.)

Chairman Borah was not alone in provoking the ire of the foreign policy elites. Consider this missive launched against his predecessor, Chairman Lodge, by the *New York Times* editorial page on July 19, 1919: "The light of truth and knowledge will penetrate the shadows of the crypt in which the Foreign Relations Committee of the Senate holds its sessions only over the prostrate form of Henry Cabot Lodge, Chairman of that Committee. The legions of light, multitudinous, bold, powerful, have by their approach startled the hosts of night in their encampment within that chamber. They storm the entrance, but there stands Lodge...unconquerable and opaque at the door of the Committee room...."

Clearly the Senate Foreign Relations Committee began rankling folks up at the *New York Times* and the Council on Foreign Relations long before I took the helm.

The *Times* editorialist who wrote that passage was frustrated with Chairman Lodge because of his opposition to the League of Nations. This is not surprising. The Senate Foreign Relations Committee has always been a source of frustration for utopian idealists in a rush to remake the world. And this, I believe, is exactly what our Founding Fathers intended. The Senate is slow to action by design, a brake on impulsive instincts. And the Foreign Relations Committee was, I believe, intended to be the Senate's brake on foreign policy.

The committee's role is contemplative; it is our job to say to presidents and secretaries of state, when they come demanding quick action on "urgent" treaties and legislation, "Slow down; let's think on this a little." We hold hearings; we listen to witnesses with differing points of view. Then, sometimes, our job is to work with an administration to improve its proposals. And sometimes our job is to say no.

Needless to say, this has been frustrating to generations of American presidents. Woodrow Wilson, for example, loathed the United States Senate. He was a man in a hurry, with grand visions of a new world order, and the Senate Foreign Relations Committee stood in his way (thank goodness!).

As a twenty-two-year-old senior at Princeton University, Wilson wrote an essay called "Congressional Government," in which he took the Founding Fathers to task for their lack of wisdom in establishing a constitutional separation of powers and heaped scorn on the Senate's power over treaties and appointments. Wilson advocated instead the adoption of a cabinet system based on the British parliamentary model—in effect, a legislative rubber stamp.

The young Mr. Wilson then sent his effort around to see if he could publish it and make a name for himself. Eventually it caught the eye of a twenty-nine-year-old Harvard lecturer, who thought it was well argued. He published it in a journal he edited, *International Review*, and that started off Woodrow Wilson's career.

The Harvard tutor was none other than Henry Cabot Lodge. And some years later, when Wilson was president and Lodge was chairman, Lodge gave President Wilson a lesson in "congressional government."

President Wilson probably could have achieved ratification of the League of Nations if he had not approached the Senate with such disdain. Chairman Lodge proposed fourteen conditions, few of which would raise an eyebrow today: language to ensure that the United States be the judge of its own internal affairs; that the United States retain the right to withdraw from the League; that the League not restrict any individual rights of U.S. citizens; that the United States assume no obligation to deploy forces through the League without approval of Congress; that Congress approve all U.S. officials appointed to the League; and that Congress control all appropriations of U.S. funds for the League. Not controversial stuff.

But President Wilson refused even to consider such reservations, howling: "Never, never! I'll never consent to adopt any policy with which that impossible man is so prominently identified." Wilson lost the final vote 38 to 53.

The lesson is this: Presidents rarely win when they refuse to work with the Senate Foreign Relations Committee. By contrast, when they have dealt with the committee in partnership, rather than confrontation, they have seen many successes.

Compare the fight over the League of Nations with the Senate's more recent consideration of NATO expansion. The growth of the Atlantic alliance is the most important foreign policy matter to come before the Senate since the end of the Cold War. Yet, while the debate was spirited, it was not confrontational. Why?

Early in the process the Foreign Relations Committee raised a number of reservations about the administration's approach to NATO expansion. For example, Dr. Henry Kissinger came and testified before the committee about his concern that by giving Russia a voice in NATO decision making, we were letting the fox into the henhouse. And so the committee drafted conditions in the Resolution of Ratification that built a "fire wall" in the NATO-Russia relationship. Also, over the next nine months, my fellow committee members and I worked with the secretary of state to address a number of other concerns. The result? The Senate overwhelmingly approved NATO expansion. Had the administration dug in its heels and expected the committee to rubber-stamp the expansion protocols, I can assure you the Senate would still be deliberating the wisdom of NATO expansion today.

So I disagree with President Wilson: I believe the Founding Fathers showed great wisdom when they established the separation of powers. Because in so doing, they ensured a voice for the American people in their nation's foreign policy—a check on those foreign policy elites who would prefer to run foreign affairs unencumbered by the popular will.

The Founders understood what President Wilson did not: that there is wisdom in the American heartland. They trusted in that wisdom. And senators who serve on the Foreign Relations Committee must never forget what a privileged role the American people have granted us by allowing us to be their voice in the great debates over the security of our nation.

Chapter 2
International *"Justice"*

SHOULD THE UNITED STATES OF AMERICA allow its citizens to come under the jurisdiction of a United Nations "International Criminal Court"?

Most of the world thinks we should. But in 1998, as delegates from around the world gathered in Rome to negotiate a treaty establishing such a court, Senator Helms laid down a marker: Any treaty that would allow this international court to try an American citizen, he said, would be "dead on arrival" in the Senate Foreign Relations Committee.

Senator Helms saw this proposed court as a dangerous threat to American sovereignty, a tool for politicized prosecutions of American citizens, and a threat to continued U.S. engagement in the world.

Although he did not go to Rome, Senator Helms's shadow hung over the treaty conference. The Clinton administration supported the International Criminal Court in principle and badly wanted to sign the treaty, but Senator Helms's declaration constrained U.S. delegates from making dangerous concessions. In large part because of its inability to address his objections and get a "ratifiable" treaty, the administration was unable to sign the Rome treaty.

Nonetheless, the treaty was approved without the United States. And, amazingly, the delegates decided to give the court the power to try virtually anyone—even American citizens—whether or not the United States has signed, or the Senate ratified, the Rome treaty.

Soon after the conference, former Chilean president Augusto Pinochet was arrested in London on a warrant by a Spanish judge seeking to try him in Spain for "crimes against humanity"—over the objections of Chile's democratically elected government. For Senator Helms, this outrageous act confirmed all his earlier warnings about this arbitrary and capricious new system of "international justice."

In these essays, Senator Helms explains his objections to the International Criminal Court—why the United States cannot simply ignore it but rather must actively work to stop it, and why the efforts to extradite General Pinochet, and overrule Chile's national reconciliation process, show how this new system of international "justice" is a danger that must be contained.

~~~~~~~

SLAY THIS MONSTER
Financial Times, July 30, 1998

THE DECISION BY THE UNITED STATES to walk away from the Rome treaty establishing a United Nations International Criminal Court was clearly the right thing to do. Since the signing ceremony in Rome, however, several governments have made clear their belief that the United States will eventually succumb to international pressure and join the court, while others are hopeful that we will simply look the other way and not interfere with the efforts to establish and legitimize the court. The United States can afford to do neither.

Rejecting the Rome treaty is not enough. The United States must fight the treaty. Lloyd Axworthy, Canadian foreign minister, asked a good question in Rome: "The question is whether [the United States] treats [the court] with benign neglect, or whether they are aggressively opposed." We must be aggressively opposed, because, even if the United States never joins the court, the Rome treaty will have serious implications for U.S. foreign policy.

The Rome treaty is an irreparably flawed and dangerous document. It includes as one of its "core crimes" something called "aggression"—a crime that was included even though the countries negotiating the treaty were unable to reach agreement on just what it is. Yet it seems clear that this court will consider it a crime of aggression whenever America takes any military action to defend its national interests unless the United States first seeks and receives the permission of the UN.

This court proposes to sit in judgment on U.S. national security policy. Imagine what would have happened if this court had been in place during the U.S. invasion of Panama. Or the U.S. invasion of Grenada. Or the U.S. bombing of Tripoli. In none of those cases did the United States seek permission from the UN to defend our interests. And so long as there is breath in me, the United States will never—I repeat, never—allow its national security decisions to be judged by an International Criminal Court.

Anyone who doubts that the court will attempt to do so need only look to recent history. In the 1980s the World Court attempted to declare that U.S. support for the Nicaraguan Contras was in violation of international law. The Reagan administration wisely ignored the World Court because it lacked jurisdiction and so had no authority in that matter.

Well, the International Criminal Court declares that the American people are under its jurisdiction—no matter what the U.S. government says. The delegates in Rome included a form of "universal jurisdiction" in the court statute, which means that, even if the United States never signs the treaty, or if the Senate refuses to ratify it, the countries participating in this court will still contend that American soldiers and citizens are within the jurisdiction of the court.

That is an outrage—and will have grave consequences for our relations with every country that signs and ratifies this treaty.

Consider: Germany was the intellectual author of this universal jurisdiction provision. The United States has thousands of soldiers stationed in Germany. Will the German government now consider those forces under the jurisdiction of the International Criminal Court? I support keeping our forces in Germany—but not if Germany insists on exposing them to the jurisdiction of the ICC.

Indeed, the Clinton administration will now have to renegotiate the status of our forces agreements not only with Germany but also with every other signatory state where American soldiers are stationed. And we must make clear to these governments that their refusal to do so will force us to reconsider our ability to station forces on their territory, participate in peacekeeping operations, and meet our Article Five commitments under the NATO charter.

This treaty also represents a massive dilution of the authority of the UN Security Council—and the U.S. veto within the council. In the words of the Indian representative, the delegates in Rome decided that "any preeminent role of the Security Council [would] constitute a violation of sovereign equality... [because] the composition of the Security Council and the veto vested in five permanent members is an anomaly which cannot be reproduced and recognized by the International Criminal Court."

Incredibly, during the negotiations the United States went along with this backdoor effort to dilute the Security Council's powers, agreeing to a proposal by Singapore that turns the Security Council on its head. Under the treaty adopted in Rome, the United States cannot veto a case going before the court. Rather, blocking a case will require the support of a majority of the council, as well as consensus among all the permanent members. Such a dilution of veto power in the Security Council is unacceptable and must be fought by the United States.

Because this court has such wide-ranging implications for the United States, even if we are never a party to the treaty, I intend to seek assurances from the Clinton administration that:

- The United States will never vote in the Security Council to refer a case to the court.

- The United States will provide no assistance whatsoever to the court, either in funding, in-kind contributions, or other legal assistance.

- The United States will not extradite any individual to the court or, directly or indirectly, refer a case to the court.

- The United States will include in all of its bilateral extradition treaties a provision prohibiting a treaty partner from extraditing U.S. citizens to this court.

- The United States will renegotiate every one of its status-of-forces agreements to include a provision that prohibits a treaty partner from extraditing U.S. soldiers to this court—and will not station forces in any country that refuses to accept such a prohibition.

- The United States will not permit a U.S. soldier to participate in any NATO, UN, or other international peacekeeping mission until the United States has reached agreement with all of our NATO allies and the UN that no U.S. soldier will be subject to the jurisdiction of this court.

The International Criminal Court is a threat to U.S. national interests. We cannot treat it with the "benign neglect" Mr. Axworthy is hoping for. As a Dutch delegate put it at the conclusion, "I won't say we gave birth to a monster, but the baby has some defects."

He is wrong. The ICC is indeed a monster—and it is our responsibility to slay it before it grows to haunt us.

AND AFTER PINOCHET?
Washington Post, **December 10, 1998**

DURING THE ROME CONFERENCE to establish an International Criminal Court, I warned that such a court would be arbitrary and contemptuous of national judicial processes and would trample the sovereignty of democratic nations.

The delegates and "human rights" activists in Rome scoffed at my concerns. The new system of international justice, they promised, would never allow a rogue prosecutor, answerable to no government or institution, to interfere with the national reconciliation process of a stable democracy with a functioning legal system. Only dictatorships would be affected.

Well, follow their deeds, not their words. The treatment of former Chilean president Augusto Pinochet has confirmed my every warning.

Today a rogue Spanish judge is using "international law" to trample Chilean sovereignty and overrule Chile's functioning judiciary, its democratically elected government, and the decision of its people to choose national reconciliation over revenge. And the advocates of the International Criminal Court are cheering him along.

Amnesty International USA president William Schulz fired off a letter to Secretary of State Madeleine Albright last week stating that Amnesty was "deeply concerned about statements you made in which you imply that the decision whether or not to extradite Pinochet should be left to the Chilean people." (Heaven forfend!) "Your statement," he continues, "is akin to stating that... Pinochet should not be extradited to Spain." In other words, Amnesty acknowledges that the Chilean people and their elected leaders oppose Pinochet's extradition; it just doesn't care. The Pinochet case should sound alarm bells for citizens of every democratic nation. It puts the integrity of our judicial systems and right to self-government in danger.

Much has been said of human rights abuses during the Pinochet era. I do not condone abuses by anyone. But the majority of Chileans will tell you that the 1973 coup d'état led by Pinochet rescued their country from ruinous anarchy. His action stopped Chile's transformation into a Cuban-style communist state and the spread of Marxist revolution across Latin America.

And what is beyond dispute is that in 1988 Pinochet voluntarily submitted his rule to a national plebiscite and then respected the results of that popular vote by stepping down and handing power to a democratically elected civilian president. He left Chile a free, thriving, prosperous democratic nation.

The Chilean people took stock of Pinochet's legacy—both the success and excesses of his regime—and made a conscious decision to move on. Some may disagree with this, but it was a decision for the Chilean people alone to make.

Now comes Baltasar Garzon, who has arbitrarily decided he will overrule their decision. Okay, if overruling Chile's national reconciliation is acceptable, how about South Africa? The Truth and Reconciliation Commission just declared that the African National Congress committed gross violations of human rights, including torture, assassination, and summary execution of hundreds of political opponents. ANC leaders all received amnesty. Should some foreign judge now have the power to over-rule that decision and force them to stand trial?

The new system of global "justice" being created here is arbitrary and capricious. The same day that Pinochet was arrested in London, Spain's prime minister was clinking glasses with Fidel Castro at the Ibero-American summit. Yet when Cuban exiles petitioned Garzon's court to begin similar proceedings against Castro, he contemptuously dismissed their case.

If Castro goes free, how about Gorbachev? Under his leadership, the Soviet Union committed genocidal acts, war crimes, and crimes against humanity in Afghanistan and sent KGB death squads into Latvia and Lithuania. Should Gorbachev be arrested on his next speaking tour?

Jiang Zemin travels freely between the capitals of Europe. Why not arrest him and prosecute him for the thousands he murdered in Tiananmen Square? Why not arrest Yasser Arafat for acts of terrorism he ordered?

The point is this: Who decides who stands trial and who goes free in this brave new world of "global justice"? Some self-appointed Spanish judge? Some foreign prosecutor in an International Criminal Court? Or the free peoples of sovereign democratic nations?

Garzon and his allies counter that they are putting dictators on notice that justice now reaches across borders. Dictators will be put on notice, all right. And the lesson will be: Never step down—you'd be a fool to give up power, as Pinochet did. Fight until the last man.

I would gladly trade Fidel Castro a comfortable exile in Spain for his decision to step down and allow Cubans to live in freedom. But if Garzon succeeds, there will be no more "peaceful transitions to democracy." If dictators cannot be offered amnesty or safety in exile, they will never hand power to democratic movements. The incentive will be for greater repression, not less.

This is the world that crusaders for the International Criminal Court are unwittingly creating. The United States must actively oppose it.

WHY ISRAEL MUST NOT SIGN THE ICC TREATY
Ha'aretz, December 17, 2000

ARAB FOREIGN MINISTERS meeting in Cairo in October issued a scathing communiqué accusing Israel of massacring innocent Palestinian civilians. To redress these Israeli "war crimes" they called for the establishment of an international tribunal to investigate and punish Israel.

The Arab League communiqué declared: "The Arab leaders... call upon the Security Council to set up a special international criminal court for the trial of Israeli war criminals, who committed massacres against the Palestinians and Arabs in the occupied territories, on the pattern of the two courts that have been set up by the council to try war criminals in Rwanda and former Yugoslavia."

The Arab leaders were well aware that nothing would come of their call for a war crimes tribunal. The only way to set up a tribunal like the ones for Rwanda and Yugoslavia is through a UN Security Council resolution. And they knew full well that the United States has a Security Council veto and would use it without hesitation to block the creation of a politicized court to go after Israel.

But imagine for a moment a world in which the United States is stripped of that veto. Imagine that launching a war crimes prosecution against Israel did not require a Security Council resolution at all—and that all that was needed for Israel's enemies to open an international criminal investigation of Israeli soldiers, military officials, and political leaders was to convince just one, independent international prosecutor, answerable to no government or institution for his actions, to issue the indictments. Imagine if the United States was powerless to stop that prosecutor from going after Israel.

In other words, imagine the world with an International Criminal Court!

In 1998 a UN conference in Rome approved a treaty establishing a permanent International Criminal Court. Such a court, in theory, sounds like a dream come true—the culmination of a process begun in Nuremberg to end forever impunity for the most heinous crimes of war. But in fact, the court that emerged in Rome is not a dream, but a nightmare.

A total of 116 countries signed the Rome treaty, but the United States and Israel refused. (It is not a coincidence that the two democracies that refused to sign—the United States and Israel—are also the two nations in the world most likely to suffer politicized prosecutions in this dangerously flawed court.)

The International Criminal Court claims jurisdiction to try and imprison American and Israeli citizens—including our military personnel and government officials—even if our governments have not signed or ratified the Rome treaty. The International Criminal Court will have the power to indict, prosecute, *and imprison* persons virtually anywhere in the world accused by the court of "war crimes," "crimes against humanity," and "genocide"—as well as an as yet to be defined crime of "aggression." (Mark my words: "Aggression" will be defined as any time the United States or Israel takes military action to defend our territory, our citizens, or our vital national interests.)

The court will have an independent prosecutor answerable to no state or institution for his or her actions. Why is this dangerous? Imagine what might happen if the Court existed at this very moment. The International Criminal Court prosecutor could—without consulting the Security Council or any other balancing authority—respond to the Arab League request by issuing criminal indictments against Israeli soldiers, military commanders, and government officials all the way up to the prime minister himself.

The *only* way Israel could stop the prosecutor from going forward would be for the Israeli government to agree to take up the investigations on its own. The Israeli Justice Ministry would then be in the position of having to conduct criminal investigations of its own prime minister, senior officials, and soldiers in order to placate the court. Assuming that Israel found these individuals were not guilty of any crimes, a three-judge panel of this International Criminal Court could still overrule the Israeli government and allow the prosecutor to proceed with the indictments. From that moment on, the indicted servicemen and officials could never set foot outside Israeli territory—any signatory nation would be under a treaty obligation to arrest them and send them to the Hague to stand trial.

Think the court would not go after Israel? Think again. On October 27, just days after the Arab League declaration condemning Israel, the United Nations Human Rights Commission approved a resolution finding that "the deliberate and systematic killing of civilians and children by the Israeli occupying authorities constitutes a flagrant and grave violation of the right to life... and also constitutes a war crime and a crime against humanity." If the court were in place today, such a resolution would virtually guarantee an indictment by the independent prosecutor.

And even before the Rome treaty was signed, the nations forming the International Criminal Court already were using it to attack Israel. They included as a so-called "crime" the transfer of civilians of an "occupying power" into an "occupied territory"—a clear attack on Israel's settlement policy.

In Rome, the United States attempted to insert checks and balances on the prosecutor's unbridled discretion by requiring a Security Council "screen" that would permit the United States to veto cases from going forward. This was flatly rejected. And in the two years since the Rome conference, the delegates have rebuffed U.S. efforts to secure real, concrete protections that would restrain the independent prosecutor from engaging in politicized prosecutions of our servicemen and officials.

This International Criminal Court is a clear and present danger to Israel and the United States. That is why, last month, more than a dozen former senior American officials—including former secretaries of state and defense, national security advisors, directors of Central Intelligence, and UN ambassadors representing every administration going back to Nixon—together signed a letter opposing the International Criminal Court.

The letter, whose signatories included Henry Kissinger, Jeane Kirkpatrick, George Shultz, and James Woolsey, declared that the International Criminal Court is a "threat to American sovereignty and international freedom of action" and stated that "the president, cabinet officers, and other senior national security decision makers [should] not have to fear international criminal prosecution as they go about their work. The risk of international criminal prosecution will certainly chill decision-making within our government, and could limit the willingness of our national leadership to respond forcefully to acts of terrorism, aggression and other threat to American interests."

Despite what these officials call the court's "obvious defects," both Israel and the United States are coming under intense pressure this month to change their positions and sign the Rome statute before the end of the year. The United States and Israel must resist this pressure.

It is understandably difficult for Israel to remain outside of the court. Few peoples in history are as intimately familiar with the concepts of genocide and crimes against humanity as the Jewish people. For a court that claims to be the successor to the Nuremberg tribunal to proceed without the participation of the Jewish state surely must make many in Israel uncomfortable. Indeed, Israeli diplomats have confided to me that one of the Barak government's last acts may be to sign the Rome treaty.

But both the politicians and the people of Israel must understand that this court is *not* the successor to the Nuremberg court. The International Criminal Court is the League of Nations of international justice—a flawed first attempt to create a permanent tribunal that, when it goes awry, could forever undermine the credibility of international justice.

Some have suggested that Israel can protect itself by signing, but not ratifying, the Rome statute. This is no solution. First, signing treaties that one has no intention of abiding by is how lawless dictatorships, not law-abiding democracies, behave. Second, the International Criminal Court ultimately will not require Israeli ratification in order to assert criminal jurisdiction over Israeli actions. If any state bordering Israel ratifies the Rome statute—including the potential Palestinian state—the International Criminal Court will have jurisdiction to prosecute Israeli soldiers operating on the territory of that state, as well as officials of the Israeli government who direct them. Once such a situation emerges, as it surely will, Israel's only real defense against the court will be to reject its legitimacy. This will be far more difficult, both legally and politically, if Israel has signed the Rome statute than if it has not. Finally, by signing the Rome statute Israel would be signaling its approval of this dangerously flawed treaty and would undermine efforts to protect our citizens from the jurisdiction of the court.

Israel will gain no additional procedural or substantive rights by signing the Rome statute now. But by signing, Israel will lose its right to question the International Criminal Court's legitimacy when, inevitably, the court caves in to Arab pressure to prosecute Israeli soldiers and government officials.

As painful as it must be, Israel must stand firm and refuse to sign the Rome treaty. The United States and Israel have supported the ad hoc tribunals established through existing Security Council procedures and can continue to do so in the future. But Israel will rue the day it lends its signature and credibility to this irreparably flawed court.

Any Israeli who is tempted to sign should first turn on the evening news and take a good, hard look at those brave Israeli soldiers defending themselves against rock-throwing mobs of Palestinians—and consider that those soldiers are the "war criminals" this court will one day seek to prosecute.

Chapter 3

The Dysfunctional United Nations

WHEN IT COMES TO DYSFUNCTIONAL INTERNATIONAL INSTITUTIONS, the United Nations is the poster child. For this reason, Senator Helms has made it his mission to press for dramatic reforms at the United Nations.

When Senator Helms took charge of the Foreign Relations Committee in 1995, the United Nations (under then–secretary-general Boutros Boutros-Ghali) was spinning out of control—growing in cost and seeking new powers to collect taxes and raise a standing UN army. The United States and the UN were in a standoff over America's so-called UN "arrears," accrued under the outgoing Democratic Congress, which had withheld a small portion of America's UN dues each year as pressure to curtail the rampant waste, fraud, and abuse at the UN.

In the first of these essays, Senator Helms takes Boutros-Ghali to task for his campaign of "UN empowerment." Instead of seeking to expand the UN's powers and authorities, Helms writes, the secretary-general should be downsizing the UN and limiting its scope and mission. The second essay, written for *Foreign Affairs* magazine before Boutros-Ghali's ouster, is a manifesto for UN reform addressed to his as yet unnamed successor.

Under pressure from Helms and other Senate Republicans, the Clinton administration decided to replace Boutros-Ghali with a more reform-minded secretary-general—Kofi Annan. When Annan took office, Senator Helms immediately invited him to Washington and made him an offer: Helms would lead the charge to pay the UN arrears if Annan would agree to implement a series of specific reform benchmarks.

Helms immediately began work on bipartisan legislation to fulfill his end of the commitment—the "Helms-Biden" law. A grand "arrears-for-reform" bargain seemed assured. But the issue soon became embroiled in the Clinton impeachment scandal. Under pressure from "women's groups" (who were threatening to abandon him over the scandal), the president threatened to veto the bill over a single provision included by House Republicans that barred taxpayer subsidies for groups that lobby foreign governments to legalize abortion.

As incredible as it seemed, the president was willing to veto a bipartisan effort to settle the UN arrears in order to preserve federal subsidies for foreign abortion lobbying. In a *New York Times* essay—published as Clinton prepared to address the UN General Assembly and as the House considered articles of impeachment—Senator Helms challenged the president and informed UN delegates that Clinton had the power that day to pay the UN arrears with the stroke of his pen.

The president did veto the bill. But a year later, as the Lewinsky episode faded from the national spotlight, Congress passed the Helms-Biden bill again. And this time, the president signed the legislation—virtually unchanged from the version he had vetoed the year before—into law.

With the Helms-Biden law passed, Senator Helms led the Foreign Relations Committee on a historic visit to the United Nations. The committee held a field hearing on UN reform—the first time a Senate committee had traveled as a group to visit an international institution. And Senator Helms became the first legislator in history to address the United Nations Security Council. In a speech that pulled no punches but at the same time extended a hand in friendship to the UN, he called for all parties to work together to turn a new page in U.S.-UN relations.

Helms also invited the UN Security Council to come to Washington as the guests of the Foreign Relations Committee, which they did several months later. A historic dialogue had begun.

As 2000 came to a close, Senator Helms's strategy was vindicated when the UN member states agreed (with a great deal of arm-twisting from Ambassador Richard Holbrooke) to implement virtually all of the reforms required in the Helms-Biden law.

Speaking on the Senate floor after the agreement, Senator Biden delivered a remarkable tribute to Senator Helms, declaring, "Just as only Nixon could go to China, only Helms could fix the UN."

MR. BOUTROS-GHALI HAS TO CHANGE HIS TUNE
Washington Times, February 23, 1996

THE APOSTLE PAUL TOLD THE ROMANS that almost they per-
suadeth him, but the gentleman who serves as secretary-general of
the United Nations needs much more practice before he is likely
to gain sympathy for the UN's plight, as Boutros Boutros-Ghali
described it the other day.

The United Nations, he declared a tad mournfully in a speech
to the "High Level Working Group on the Financial Situation of
the UN," is on the verge of bankruptcy. The secretary-general is
a cordial man, but his Henny Penny declarations probably will not
be persuasive to those who inhabit the real world.

Any organization facing bankruptcy must stop spending money
it doesn't have and must look for ways to slash its budget, cut
bureaucracy, and eliminate waste. But not the UN. Not only did
Mr. Boutros-Ghali fail in his speech to put forward even one single new idea for serious UN reform, he could not bring himself to
endorse even the meager 10 percent cut in the massive UN
bureaucracy proposed by Undersecretary-General Joseph Conner.

Why was the secretary-general unwilling to accept even minor
reductions? Because Mr. Boutros-Ghali rejects the advice that the
monstrous UN bureaucracy must be pared down and the scope
of the United Nations' activities cut back. To the contrary, the
secretary-general's agenda has always been, as he puts it, to
"empower the UN." What he is really after is much more than
just fast cash to stave off supposed bankruptcy. What Mr. Boutros-
Ghali really wants is the power to collect his own taxes.

The secretary-general signaled his intentions in a speech at
Oxford University last month, in which he laid out proposed UN

taxes on, among other things, international financial transactions, global currency transactions, fossil fuel use, international travel, and travel documents. And he declared in no uncertain terms, "It will be the role of the secretary-general to bring this project to fruition in the twenty-first century."

The secretary-general's tax proposal is part of his stated agenda for establishing a level of "independence" for the UN secretariat from the political and financial will of the member states—an agenda that must be, and surely will be, forcefully rejected by the United States.

What the secretary-general really means by UN "independence," many have come to believe, is UN "sovereignty." Indeed, Mr. Boutros-Ghali has often stated his view that the sovereignty of nations is an outdated concept. In his 1992 *Agenda for Peace*, Mr. Boutros-Ghali declared: "The time of absolute and exclusive sovereignty...has passed. Its theory was never matched by reality. It is the task of leaders of States today to understand this." In his view, UN member nations—including the United States—should be willing to cede a measure of their sovereignty to the United Nations.

Consider: Only sovereign entities have standing armies or the powers of taxation; the secretary-general has proposed both for the United Nations. Mr. Boutros-Ghali has long advocated the establishment of a standing UN military, and in 1992 he presented a report to the United Nations in which he argued for the creation of just such a permanent UN force—a proposal that remains on his long-term agenda. Now he is pushing for the power to tax. When asked by a BBC interviewer whether "the United Nations could raise taxes around the world as though it were a government," the secretary-general unhesitatingly declared, "Yes."

The UN is not a government, it has no sovereignty, and the trend toward UN "independence" is one that the United States will ignore at its peril. For this reason, objections to proposals such as Mr. Boutros-Ghali's UN power to tax must be voiced loudly, clearly, and immediately. That is why Senator Bob Dole and I responded to the secretary-general's idea by introducing legislation that will cut off all U.S. funding to the United Nations if and when it seeks to impose such a scheme—to send an unmistakable message to the UN bureaucrats in New York that under no circumstances will the Congress of the United States allow them to gain the powers of taxation over American citizens.

Ideas like this proposed power to tax are what give the United Nations a bad name with the American people, who rightly perceive such measures as power grabbing by international bureaucrats. Today, when Americans look at the United Nations, what they see is a bureaucratic monster, impervious to reform, claiming more and more of their resources to fund a wasteful international bureaucracy; they see an emerging world government that yearns to tax them without representation and to send their children to fight and die in foreign adventures that bear no relation to U.S. national interests. Proposals for UN taxes and a UN military, and chiding the United States as a "deadbeat nation," do nothing to change this negative public opinion.

The reality that Mr. Boutros-Ghali does not want to face is that the United Nations does not have a revenue problem; it has a spending problem. Congress has refused to continue giving the United Nations American tax dollars hand over fist because of the UN's stubborn refusal to enact real reform.

Congress must make clear its insistence on wide-scale UN reform—a reform that requires, as a price for continued U.S. participation, a dramatic downsizing of the scope and activities of the United Nations. As a starting point, the United States should insist on some minimum changes in the UN's structure, charter, and activities, including:

- An end to world government proposals such as a UN power to tax and a UN military.

- An amendment to the UN Charter reaffirming respect for the "absolute and exclusive sovereignty" of member nations.

- A 50 percent cut in the bloated UN bureaucracy.

- An end to unnecessary UN specialized agencies, making all UN agencies voluntary so that member states can decide their own levels of participation.

- An end to lavish UN conferences such as the Beijing women's summit and the upcoming Habitat II conference, for which American taxpayers are forced to pay millions of dollars to promote an agenda the vast majority of them do not support.

- A restoration of absolute U.S. control over American contributions to the United Nations, ensuring that the U.S. Congress, and not the UN General Assembly, decide how much—if anything—we contribute to the United Nations. (Today, the UN can spend as it sees fit and then demand that the United States pay a percentage of its budget. This is unacceptable.)

If the United Nations refuses to enact such reforms, it will be sowing the seeds of its own demise. No public institution can long endure without at least a modicum of popular support. If the secretary-general feels obliged to dream, let him dream not of taxes and armies but of reform. A sovereign United Nations may be the stuff Mr. Boutros-Ghali's dreams are made of, but for Americans it is a recurring nightmare that bodes the collapse of U.S. support for the United Nations.

SAVING THE UN
Foreign Affairs, September–October 1996

NOT LONG AGO, while accompanying UN ambassador Madeleine Albright to an appearance in North Carolina, I was asked by a reporter whether the United States should withdraw from the United Nations. It was a valid question. I responded, "Not yet."

As it currently operates, the United Nations does not deserve continued American support. Its bureaucracy is proliferating, its costs are spiraling, and its mission is constantly expanding beyond its mandate—and beyond its capabilities. Worse, with the steady growth in the size and scope of its activities, the United Nations is being transformed from an institution of sovereign nations into a quasi-sovereign entity in itself. That transformation represents an obvious threat to U.S. national interests. Worst of all, it is a transformation that is being funded principally by American taxpayers. The United States contributes more than $3.5 billion every year to the UN system as a whole, making it the most generous benefactor of this power-hungry and dysfunctional organization.

This situation is untenable. The United Nations needs to be radically overhauled. Yet Secretary-General Boutros Boutros-Ghali has ignored multiple warnings and stubbornly resisted reform that gets down to fundamentals. On the contrary, Boutros-Ghali has pursued a well-publicized campaign of what he calls

UN "empowerment." He has protected the bloated bureaucracy, and the number and nature of peacekeeping operations has vastly expanded under his tenure. He has pressed for the establishment of a standing UN army and the power to collect direct UN taxes.

Now, with UN "empowerment" as his platform, Boutros-Ghali has reversed his pledge to serve a single term and is seeking a second one. The Clinton administration has belatedly announced its opposition but has failed to nominate or even search for a replacement, just as it has been complacent in the face of his presumptions to power.

Rather than Boutros-Ghali's "empowerment," the United Nations needs a stark reassessment of its mission and its mandate. The next secretary-general must help develop a bold plan to cut back the overgrown bureaucracy and limit its activities, then muster the political will and leadership to implement it. The reformist zeal of the next secretary-general will in all likelihood determine whether or not the United Nations survives into the next century. For if such a plan is not put forward and implemented, the next UN secretary-general could—and should—be the last.

The United Nations was originally created to help nation-states facilitate the peaceful resolution of international disputes. However, the United Nations has moved from facilitating diplomacy among nation-states to supplanting them altogether. The international elites running the United Nations look at the idea of the nation-state with disdain; they consider it a discredited notion of the past that has been superseded by the idea of the United Nations. In their view, the interests of nation-states are parochial and should give way to global interests. Nation-states, they believe, should recognize the primacy of these global interests and accede to the UN's sovereignty to pursue them.

Boutros-Ghali has said as much. In his 1992 *Agenda for Peace*, he declared his view that the sovereignty of nations is an outdated concept: "The time of absolute and exclusive sovereignty...has passed. Its theory was never matched by reality. It is the task of leaders of states to understand this." In other words, UN member nations, including the United States, should be willing to abandon claims of "absolute and exclusive sovereignty" and empower the United Nations by ceding it a measure of their sovereignty. They should give the secretary-general a standing army and the power to collect taxes—functions that legitimately rest only with sovereign states.

Such thinking is in step with the nearly global movement toward greater centralization of political power in the hands of elites at the expense of individuals and their local representatives. In the United States, Europe, and elsewhere, political leaders are belatedly recognizing the destructive effects of central bureaucracies and state-controlled economic activities and are fighting uphill battles to bring these into check. They are finding, however, that, once established, bureaucracies (along with the goodies they dispense) are nearly impossible to dismantle. As the millennium approaches, this virus of centralization is spreading to the global level, and the United Nations is its carrier. Just as massive bureaucracies have taken hold in Europe and the United States, the UN bureaucracy has established a foothold on the international stage.

This process must be stopped. In the United States, Congress has begun a process of devolution, taking power away from the federal government and returning it to the states. This must be replicated at the international level. Reining in the UN bureaucracy goes hand in hand with Congress's domestic agenda of devolution. UN reform is about much more than saving money. It is about preventing unelected bureaucrats from acquiring ever greater powers at the expense of elected national leaders. It is about restoring the legitimacy of the nation-state.

How big is the problem? According to the latest official UN statistics, the organization is home to 53,744 bureaucrats, comprising the Secretariat bureaucracy and those of the diverse specialized agencies. Hard as it is to believe, some advocates of the United Nations argue that it is not big enough. In his book *Divided It Stands: Can the United Nations Work?*, James Holtje writes that "when one considers that... [the United Nations is] expected to meet the needs of 5.5 billion people worldwide, the number begins to look small." It is not the job of the United Nations to "meet the needs" of 5.5 billion people—that is the job of nation-states.

But the UN bureaucracy mistakenly believes that caring for the needs of all the world's people is exactly its job. From the bureaucracy's vantage point, there are no international, national, or even local problems—all problems are UN problems. Thus we have the recent Habitat II conference in Istanbul, where the United Nations spent millions of dollars to address the concerns of cities—an issue that legitimately should be handled by local or national governments.

So what is wrong with the United Nations' lending a helping hand on these matters? The issue is not just sticking the UN's nose where it does not belong. By making every problem its problem, the United Nations often makes the situation worse. Instead of helping nation-states solve problems, the United Nations does the exact opposite—it creates a disincentive for states to handle problems that are their responsibility to resolve. When every local or regional problem becomes a global one, the buck stops nowhere. Solving it becomes everyone's responsibility, and thus no one's responsibility.

The war in Bosnia is a perfect example. Dealing with Serbia's illegal aggression and genocide in Bosnia was the responsibility of the European powers, in whose region the crisis lay, and of the United States, which considers itself a European power. But instead of addressing the issue themselves, the Clinton administration and our European allies pushed responsibility for handling this problem onto the United Nations, which accepted a mission it was incapable of fulfilling. The UN peacekeeping operation became an excuse for inaction by the Europeans and Americans, who used the United Nations to pretend they were addressing the problem. As a result, thousands upon thousands of innocent civilians died, while the United Nations, through a combination of impotence and negligence, did nothing to stop the genocide.

The United Nations also complicates matters by giving states with no interest in a particular problem an excuse to meddle without putting anything concrete on the table. Countries that have no natural interest in an issue suddenly want to get involved, and the United Nations gives them the legitimacy to do so without cash or constructive contributions. What, for example, are countries like Togo, Zaire, Panama, or Ireland, or China for that matter, prepared to contribute to bringing about Middle East peace? They have no legitimate role in the peace process, save that which their UN membership (and in some cases seats on the Security Council) gives them. What the United Nations ends up doing is giving lots of countries a seat at the table that bring nothing to the table.

By making every issue a global issue, the United Nations is attempting to create a world that does not exist. A United Nations that can recognize its limitations—helping sovereign states work together where appropriate and staying out of issues where it has no legitimate role—is worth keeping; a United Nations that insists on imposing its utopian vision on states begs for dismantlement.

Successful reform would achieve the twin goals of arresting UN encroachment on the sovereignty of nation-states while harnessing a dramatically downsized United Nations to help sovereign nations cope with some cross-border problems. Such reform must begin by replacing Boutros Boutros-Ghali with a new secretary-general who will go in on day one with a daring agenda to reduce bureaucracy, limit missions, and refine objectives.

Second, there must be at least a 50 percent cut in the entire UN bureaucracy. The Clinton administration has made the standard of reform a "zero-growth" budget. This is inadequate. So long as this bureaucracy remains in place, it will continue to find new missions to justify its existence.

Third, there must be a termination of unnecessary committees and conferences. Since its founding as an organization of five organs in 1945, literally hundreds of UN agencies, commissions, committees, and subcommittees have proliferated. Today, for example, the United Nations includes a Committee on Peaceful Uses of Outer Space, which counts among its crowning achievements the passage of a resolution calling upon sovereign nations to report all contacts with extraterrestrial beings directly to the secretary-general.

In addition to massive, wasteful conferences like the Beijing women's summit and Habitat II, the United Nations continually sponsors workshops, expert consultations, technical consultations, and panel discussions—last year some seven thousand in Geneva alone. Most of these can be terminated, at a savings of millions of dollars.

Fourth, the UN budgeting process must be radically over-hauled. Budgets for UN voluntary organizations are currently amassed through a bidding process, where nation-states must make capital investments prior to involvement in specific issues or projects under UN auspices. This should be the model for the entire UN budgeting system. The secretary-general currently has a budget of roughly $1 billion to pay for the activities of the Security Council, General Assembly, Economic and Social Council, Secretariat, and International Court of Justice, plus the administrative costs of numerous relief, development, and humanitarian agencies. This budget is voted on by the General Assembly, where the United States has no veto, and where every nation—whether democratic or dictatorial, no matter how much or how little it contributes to the United Nations—has an equal vote.

This system should be abolished. Instead, the secretary-general should be limited to a bare-bones budget of some $250 million, and UN activities should be funded on a voluntary basis. This would essentially subject all UN programs to a market test. Each country would decide the value of programs by how much it was willing to pay. Those programs that were really vital would continue to receive support, while those championed only by the bureaucracy would die of malnutrition.

Some bargaining would naturally result (country X would say to country Y, You help with my project, and I'll help with yours). But this system would dramatically cut down on waste, eliminate freeloaders, empower member states vis-à-vis the bureaucracy in budget determinations, give states a voice in the UN commensurate with their willingness to pay while forcing wealthier countries to pay more, and give the United States and others the option not to fund or participate in programs they are currently compelled to support but which they feel directly violate their interests.

Lastly, peacekeeping must be overhauled. Peacekeeping is the United Nations' fastest-growing industry. In 1988 the total cost of UN peacekeeping operations around the world was just $230 million; in 1994, it was $3.6 billion. Of that, the United States was directly assessed nearly $1.2 billion, plus additional in-kind contributions of personnel, equipment, and other support totaling roughly $1.7 billion (all of which was skimmed off the U.S. defense budget).

Not only have costs proliferated, but so has the scope of peacekeeping missions. Prior to 1990 most peacekeeping missions were just that: monitoring truces, policing cease-fires, and serving as a buffer between parties. Today, however, peacekeeping has evolved into a term without meaning. It is used to justify all sorts of UN activities—everything from holding elections to feeding hungry people to nation building. As the system now works, the United States has two choices: go along with a proposed peacekeeping operation and pay 31.7 percent of the cost, or veto the mission, which we do not like to do. The system should permit a third option: allow the United States to let missions go forward without U.S. funding or participation. If others in the world want to undertake nation-building operations, there is no reason the United States should discourage them—so long as American taxpayers do not have to pay for a third of it. This would allow the United Nations to serve the purpose it was designed for: helping sovereign states coordinate collective action where the will for such action exists. And, of course, Security Council members would retain the authority to veto missions they deem wholly inappropriate.

The time has come for the United States to deliver an ultimatum: Either the United Nations reforms, quickly and dramatically, or the United States will end its participation. For too long, the Clinton administration has paid lip service to the idea of UN reform without imposing any real costs for UN failure to do so. I am convinced that without the threat of American withdrawal, nothing will change. Withholding U.S. contributions has not worked. In 1986 Congress passed the Kassebaum-Solomon bill, which said to the United Nations in clear and unmistakable terms, reform or die. That did not work. A decade later, the United

Nations has neither reformed nor died. The time has come for it to do one or the other.

Legislation has been introduced in the House of Representatives by Congressman Joe Scarborough (R-Fla.) for the United States to withdraw from the United Nations and replace it with a league of democracies. This idea has merit. If the United Nations is not clearly on the path of real reform well before the year 2000, then I believe the United States should withdraw. We must not enter the new millennium with the current UN structure in place. The United States has a responsibility to lay out what is wrong with the United Nations, what the benchmarks for adequate reform are, and what steps we are willing to take if those benchmarks are not met by a certain date.

The United Nations will certainly resist any and all reform—particularly many of the smaller and less developed members, which benefit from the current system and gain influence by selling their sovereignty to the organization. That is why the next secretary-general has an enormous job to do: His or her mandate will be nothing less than to save the United Nations from itself, prove that it is not impervious to reform, and show that it can be downsized, brought under control, and harnessed to contribute to the security needs of the twenty-first century. This is a gargantuan, and perhaps impossible, task. But if it cannot be done, then the United Nations is not worth saving. And if it is not done, I, for one, will be leading the charge for U.S. withdrawal.

A DAY TO PAY OLD DEBTS
New York Times, **September 21, 1998**

DURING HIS SPEECH BEFORE the United Nations General Assembly today, President Clinton will almost certainly try to gloss over one important fact: With one stroke of his pen, he can pay the American "arrears" to the United Nations—today.

This past April, Congress reluctantly wrote the president a check to pay up $819 million and further agreed to forgive an additional $107 million in debt that the United Nations owes the United States—a total of $926 million. The bipartisan legislation also would force much needed reform on the United Nations, including cuts in personnel, limits on spending, and a reduction of American dues from 25 to 20 percent of the regular United Nations budget.

Five months have passed since Congress passed this legislation, but the check remains uncashed. Despite agreement between Congress and the administration on the "reform for arrears" package, the president has refused to sign the legislation because he objects to one minor provision—forbidding groups that accept federal subsidies to use American tax dollars to lobby foreign governments to change their abortion laws.

That's right. To protect a few abortion advocates, President Clinton has made clear that he is willing to torpedo this legislation. The president should abandon this holier-than-thou charade. Nobody got everything he or she wanted in this bill. I compromised on some provisions in this bill, as did many other senators and representatives. So why does the president think he alone is above compromise?

Twice, the House leadership has significantly watered down the abortion language the president opposes to try and reach a compromise. The original language—which was American policy under the Reagan and Bush administrations but was later reversed by President Clinton—barred the use of federal money by groups that perform abortions abroad.

But that language is not what is in the bill now awaiting the president's signature. Last fall, in an effort to strike a deal, House leaders agreed to a watered-down restriction that does nothing more than ban the use of American tax dollars to lobby changes in foreign abortion laws.

Still the administration balked. Secretary of State Madeleine Albright objected to language in a report accompanying the bill, which she said barred American groups from attending conferences aimed at changing foreign abortion laws. But in fact the language she cited was not part of the bill and was not legally binding.

Nevertheless, in the spring, House leaders compromised again, agreeing to remove the offending part of the report. (Groups can now attend, but cannot sponsor, such conferences.) Today, the abortion language in the legislation is so limited that it represents little more than a symbolic concession to pro-life Republicans.

Yet the president doggedly continues to insist that he will not make even a symbolic concession on abortion. Clearly, Mr. Clinton is desperate to keep the support of groups like the National Organization for Women and Planned Parenthood. But is the president really so desperate that he is willing to put his political needs ahead of paying the United Nations arrears?

Consider the other important programs that the president will be discarding with a veto:

- The bill includes nearly full financing of the administration's foreign affairs budget request.

- The bill authorizes Radio Free Asia to expand to a twenty-four-hour service and creates Radio Free Iraq and Radio Free Iran.

- The bill authorizes $38 million to support the democratic resistance in Iraq.

- The bill would streamline our government's diplomatic bureaucracy by shutting down the United States Information Agency
  and the Arms Control and Disarmament Agency and bringing
  the Agency for International Development under State Department control.

This legislation is the president's last chance this year to pay the
United Nations. Congress has written the check. All that's needed
is the president's signature. And Mr. Clinton can sign the legislation today. Senate majority leader Trent Lott and I are prepared to
send the bill to the White House this afternoon.

To our friends at the United Nations, I say this: Don't com-
plain to Congress if this year passes without payment of the
arrears. The president has the check in his hand. When you see
him today, advise him to cash it.

AMERICAN SOVEREIGNTY AND
THE UNITED NATIONS
**An Address to the United Nations Security Council,
New York, January 20, 2000**

MR. PRESIDENT, DISTINGUISHED AMBASSADORS, Ladies and Gentlemen, thank you for your welcome this morning. It is an honor to be
here today and to meet with you here in the Security Council.

I understand that you have interpreters who translate the proceedings of this body into a half dozen different languages. It may
be that they have an interesting challenge today. As some of you
may have detected, I don't have a Yankee accent. I hope you have
a translator here who can speak Southern (someone who can
translate words like "y'all" and "I do declare").

It may be that one other language barrier will need to be overcome this morning. I am not a diplomat, and as such I am not fully conversant with the elegant and rarefied language of the diplomatic trade. I am an elected official, with something of a reputation for saying what I mean and meaning what I say. So I trust you will forgive me if I come across as a bit more blunt than those you are accustomed to hearing in this chamber.

I am told that this is the first time a United States senator has addressed the United Nations Security Council. I sincerely hope it will not be the last. It is important that this body have greater contact with the elected representatives of the American people and that we have greater contact with you.

In this spirit, tomorrow I will be joined here at the UN by several other members of the Senate Foreign Relations Committee. Together, we will meet with UN officials and representatives of some of your governments and will hold a committee "Field Hearing" to discuss UN reform and the prospects for improved U.S.-UN relations.

This will mark another first. Never before has the Senate Foreign Relations Committee ventured as a group from Washington to visit an international institution. I hope that it will be an enlightening experience for all of us and that you will accept this visit as a sign of our desire for a new beginning in the U.S.-UN relationship.

I hope—I intend—that my presence here today will presage future visits by designated spokesmen of the Security Council, who will come to Washington as official guests of the United States Senate and the Senate's Foreign Relations Committee, which I chair. I trust that your representatives will feel free to be as candid in Washington as I will try to be here today so that there will be hands of friendship extended in an atmosphere of understanding.

If we are to have such a new beginning, we must endeavor to understand each other better. And that is why I will share with you some of what I am hearing from the American people about the United Nations.

I am confident you have seen the public opinion polls, commissioned by UN supporters, suggesting that the UN enjoys the support of the American public. I would caution you not to put too much confidence in those polls. Since I was first elected to the Senate in 1972, I have run for reelection four times. Each time, the pollsters have confidently predicted my defeat. Each time, I am happy to confide, they have been wrong. I am pleased that, thus far, I have never won a poll or lost an election.

So, as those of you who represent democratic nations well know, public opinion polls can be constructed to tell you anything the poll takers want you to hear.

Let me share with you what the American people tell me. Since I became chairman of the Foreign Relations Committee, I have received literally thousands of letters from Americans all across the country expressing their deep frustration with this institution.

They know instinctively that the UN lives and breathes on the hard-earned money of the American taxpayers. And yet they have heard comments here in New York constantly calling the United States a "deadbeat."

They have heard UN officials declaring absurdly that countries like Fiji and Bangladesh are carrying America's burden in peacekeeping.

They see the majority of the UN members routinely voting against America in the General Assembly.

They have read the reports of the raucous cheering of the UN delegates in Rome, when U.S. efforts to amend the International Criminal Court treaty to protect American soldiers were defeated.

They read in the newspapers that, despite all the human rights abuses taking place in dictatorships across the globe, a UN "Special Rapporteur" decided his most pressing task was to investigate human rights violations in the United States—and found our human rights record wanting.

The American people hear all this, they resent it, and they have grown increasingly frustrated with what they feel is a lack of gratitude.

I won't delve into every point of frustration, but let's touch for just a moment on one—the "deadbeat" charge. Before coming here, I asked the United States General Accounting Office to assess just how much the American taxpayers contributed to the United Nations in 1999. Here is what the GAO reported to me:

Last year, the American people contributed a total of more than two and a half billion dollars to the UN system in assessments and voluntary contributions. That's pretty generous, but it's only the tip of the iceberg. The American taxpayers also spent an additional eight billion, seven hundred seventy-nine million dollars from the U.S. military budget to support various UN resolutions and peacekeeping operations around the world. Let me repeat that figure: eight billion, seven hundred seventy-nine million dollars.

That means that in 1999 alone the American people furnished eleven billion, two hundred seventy-nine million dollars to support the work of the United Nations. No other nation on earth comes even close to matching that singular investment.

So you can see why many Americans reject the suggestion that theirs is a "deadbeat" nation.

Now, I grant you, the money we spend on the UN is not charity. To the contrary, it is an investment—an investment from which the American people rightly expect a return. They expect a reformed UN that works more efficiently and that respects the sovereignty of the United States.

That is why in the 1980s Congress began withholding a fraction of our arrears as pressure for reform. And congressional pressure resulted in some worthwhile reforms, such as the creation of an independent UN inspector general and the adoption of consensus budgeting practices. But still, the arrears accumulated as the UN resisted more comprehensive reforms.

When the distinguished secretary-general, Kofi Annan, was elected, some of us in the Senate decided to try to establish a working relationship. The result is the Helms-Biden law, which President Clinton finally signed into law this past November. The product of three years of arduous negotiations and hard-fought compromises, it was approved by the U.S. Senate by an overwhelming 98-1 margin. You should read that vote as a virtually unanimous mandate for a new relationship with a reformed United Nations.

I am aware that this law does not sit well with some here at the UN. Some do not like to have reforms dictated by the U.S. Congress. Some have even suggested that the UN should reject these reforms.

But let me suggest a few things to consider:

First, as the figures I have cited clearly demonstrate, the United States is the single largest investor in the United Nations. Under the U.S. Constitution, we in Congress are the sole guardians of the American taxpayers' money. (It is our solemn duty to see that it is wisely invested.) So as the representatives of the UN's largest investors—the American people—we have not only a right but also a responsibility to insist on specific reforms in exchange for their investment.

Second, I ask you to consider the alternative. The alternative would have been to continue to let the U.S.-UN relationship spiral out of control. You would have taken retaliatory measures, such as revoking America's vote in the General Assembly. Congress would likely have responded with retaliatory measures against the UN. And the end result, I believe, would have been a breach in U.S.-UN relations that would have served the interests of no one.

Now some here may contend that the Clinton administration should have fought to pay the arrears without conditions. I assure you, had the administration done so, it would have lost.

Eighty years ago, Woodrow Wilson failed to secure congressional support for U.S. entry into the League of Nations. This administration obviously learned from President Wilson's mistakes.

Wilson probably could have achieved ratification of the League of Nations if he had worked with Congress. One of my predecessors as chairman of the Senate Foreign Relations Committee, Henry Cabot Lodge, asked for fourteen conditions to the treaty establishing the League of Nations, few of which would have raised an eyebrow today. These included language to ensure that the United States remain the sole judge of its own internal affairs, that the League not restrict any individual rights of U.S. citizens, that the Congress retain sole authority for the deployment of U.S. forces through the League, and so on.

But President Wilson indignantly refused to compromise with Senator Lodge. He shouted, "Never, never!" adding, "I'll never consent to adopting any policy with which that impossible man is so prominently identified!" What happened? President Wilson lost. The final vote in the Senate was 38 to 53, and the League of Nations withered on the vine.

Ambassador Richard Holbrooke and Secretary of State Madeleine Albright have understood from the beginning that the United Nations could not long survive without the support of the American people—and their elected representatives in Congress.

Thanks to the efforts of leaders like Ambassador Holbrooke and Secretary Albright , the present administration in Washington did not repeat President Wilson's fatal mistakes.

In any event, Congress has written a check to the United Nations for $926 million, payable upon the implementation of previously agreed-upon, commonsense reforms. Now the choice is up to the UN. I suggest that if the UN were to reject this compromise, it would mark the beginning of the end of U.S. support for the United Nations.

I don't want that to happen. I want the American people to value a United Nations that recognizes and respects their interests, and for the United Nations to value the significant contributions of the American people.

Let's be crystal clear and totally honest with each other: All of us want a more effective United Nations. But if the United Nations is to be "effective," it must be an institution that is needed by the great democratic powers of the world.

Most Americans do not regard the United Nations as an end in and of itself—they see it as just one tool in America's diplomatic arsenal. To the extent that the UN is an effective tool, the American people will support it. To the extent that it becomes an ineffective tool—or worse, a burden—the American people will cast it aside.

The American people want the UN to serve the purpose for which it was designed: They want it to help sovereign states coordinate collective action by "coalitions of the willing" (where the political will for such action exists); they want it to provide a forum where diplomats can meet and keep open channels of communication in times of crisis; and they want it to provide to the peoples of the world important services, such as peacekeeping, weapons inspections, and humanitarian relief.

This is important work. It is the core of what the UN can offer to the United States and the world. If, in the coming century, the

UN focuses on doing these core tasks well, it can thrive and will earn the support of the American people. But if the UN seeks to move beyond these core tasks, if it seeks to impose the UN's power and authority over nation-states, I guarantee that the United Nations will meet stiff resistance from the American people.

As matters now stand, many Americans sense that the UN has greater ambitions than simply being an efficient deliverer of humanitarian aid, a more effective peacekeeper, a better weapons inspector, and a more effective tool of great power diplomacy. They see the UN aspiring to establish itself as the central authority of a new international order of global laws and global governance. This is an international order the American people will not countenance.

The UN must respect national sovereignty. The UN serves nation-states, not the other way around. This principle is central to the legitimacy and ultimate survival of the United Nations, and it is a principle that must be protected.

The secretary-general recently delivered an address on sovereignty to the General Assembly, in which he declared that "the last right of states cannot and must not be the right to enslave, persecute, or torture their own citizens." The peoples of the world, he said, have "rights beyond borders."

I wholeheartedly agree.

What the secretary-general calls "rights beyond borders" we in America call "inalienable rights." We are endowed with those "inalienable rights," as Thomas Jefferson proclaimed in our Declaration of Independence, not by kings or despots but by our Creator.

The sovereignty of nations must be respected. But nations derive their sovereignty—their legitimacy—from the consent of the governed. Thus, it follows that nations can lose their legitimacy when they rule without the consent of the governed; they deservedly discard their sovereignty by brutally oppressing their people.

Slobodan Milosevic cannot claim sovereignty over Kosovo when he has murdered Kosovars and piled their bodies into mass graves. Neither can Fidel Castro claim that it is his sovereign right to oppress his people. Nor can Saddam Hussein defend his oppression of the Iraqi people by hiding behind phony claims of sovereignty.

And when the oppressed peoples of the world cry out for help, the free peoples of the world have a fundamental right to respond.

As we watch the UN struggle with this question at the turn of the millennium, many Americans are left exceedingly puzzled. Intervening in cases of widespread oppression and massive human rights abuses is not a new concept for the United States. The American people have a long history of coming to the aid of those struggling for freedom. In the United States, during the 1980s, we called this policy the "Reagan Doctrine."

In some cases, America has assisted freedom fighters around the world who were seeking to overthrow corrupt regimes. We have provided weaponry, training, and intelligence. In other cases, the United States has intervened directly. In still other cases, such as in Central and Eastern Europe, we supported peaceful opposition movements with moral, financial, and covert forms of support. In each case, however, it was America's clear intention to help bring down communist regimes that were oppressing their peoples, and thereby replace dictators with democratic governments.

The dramatic expansion of freedom in the last decade of the twentieth century is a direct result of these policies.

In none of these cases, however, did the United States ask for, or receive, the approval of the United Nations to "legitimize" its actions.

It is a fanciful notion that free peoples need to seek the approval of an international body (many of whose members are totalitarian dictatorships) to lend support to nations struggling to break the chains of tyranny and claim their inalienable, God-given rights.

The United Nations has no power to grant or decline legitimacy to such actions. They are inherently legitimate.

What the United Nations can do is help. The Security Council can, where appropriate, be an instrument to facilitate action by "coalitions of the willing," implement sanctions, and provide logistical support to states undertaking collective action.

But complete candor is imperative: The Security Council has an exceedingly mixed record in being such a facilitator. In the case of Iraq's aggression against Kuwait in the early 1990s, it performed admirably; in the more recent case of Kosovo, it was paralyzed. The UN peacekeeping mission in Bosnia was a disaster, and its failure to protect the Bosnian people from Serb genocide is well documented in a recent UN report.

And, despite its initial success in repelling Iraqi aggression, in the years since the Gulf War the Security Council has utterly failed to stop Saddam Hussein's drive to build instruments of mass murder. It has allowed him to play a repeated game of expelling UNSCOM inspection teams which included Americans and has left Saddam completely free for the past year to fashion nuclear and chemical weapons of mass destruction.

I am here to plead that from now on we all work together, learn from past mistakes, and make the Security Council a more efficient and effective tool for international peace and security. But candor compels that I reiterate this warning: The American people will never accept the claims of the United Nations to be the "sole source of legitimacy on the use of force" in the world.

But, some may respond, the U.S. Senate ratified the UN Charter fifty years ago. Yes, but in doing so we did not cede one syllable of American sovereignty to the United Nations. Under our system, when international treaties are ratified they simply become domestic U.S. law. As such, they carry no greater or lesser weight than any other domestic U.S. law. Treaty obligations can be superseded by a simple act of Congress. This was the intentional design of our Founding Fathers, who cautioned against entering into "entangling alliances."

Thus, when the United States joins a treaty organization, it holds no legal authority over us. We abide by our treaty obligations because they are the domestic law of our land and because our elected leaders have judged that the agreement serves our national interest. But no treaty or law can ever supersede the one document that all Americans hold sacred: the U.S. Constitution.

The American people do not want the United Nations to become an "entangling alliance." That is why Americans look with alarm at UN claims to a monopoly on international moral legitimacy. They see this as a threat to the God-given freedoms of the American people, a claim of political authority over America and its elected leaders without their consent.

The effort to establish a United Nations International Criminal Court is a case in point. Consider: The Rome treaty purports to hold American citizens under its jurisdiction—even when the United States has neither signed nor ratified the treaty. In other words, it claims sovereign authority over American citizens without their consent. How can the nations of the world imagine for one instant that Americans will stand by and allow such a power grab to take place?

The court's supporters argue that Americans should be willing to sacrifice some of their sovereignty for the noble cause of international justice. International law did not defeat Hitler, nor did it win the Cold War. What stopped the Nazi march across Europe, and the communist march across the world, was the principled projection of power by the world's great democracies. And that principled projection of force is the only thing that will ensure the peace and security of the world in the future.

More often than not, "international law" has been used as a make-believe justification for hindering the march of freedom. When Ronald Reagan sent American servicemen into harm's way to liberate Grenada from the hands of a communist dictatorship, the UN General Assembly responded by voting to condemn the action of the elected president of the United States as a violation of international law—and, I am obliged to add, it did so by a larger majority than when the Soviet invasion of Afghanistan was condemned by the same General Assembly!

Similarly, the U.S. effort to overthrow Nicaragua's communist dictatorship (by supporting Nicaragua's freedom fighters and mining Nicaragua's harbors) was declared by the World Court as a violation of international law.

Most recently, we learned that the chief prosecutor of the Yugoslav War Crimes Tribunal has compiled a report on possible NATO war crimes during the Kosovo campaign. At first, the prosecutor declared that it is fully within the scope of her authority to indict NATO pilots and commanders. When news of her report leaked, she backpedaled.

She realized, I am sure, that any attempt to indict NATO commanders would be the death knell for the International Criminal Court. But the very fact that she explored this possibility at all brings to light all that is wrong with this brave new world of global justice, which proposes a system in which independent prosecutors and judges, answerable to no state or institution, have unfettered power to sit in judgment of the foreign policy decisions of Western democracies.

No UN institution—not the Security Council, not the Yugoslav tribunal, not a future ICC—is competent to judge the foreign policy and national security decisions of the United States. American courts routinely refuse cases where they are asked to sit in judgment of our government's national security decisions, stating that they are not competent to judge such decisions. If we do not submit our national security decisions to the judgment of a court of the United States, why would Americans submit them to the judgment of an International Criminal Court, a continent away, comprised of mostly foreign judges elected by an international body made up of the membership of the UN General Assembly?

Americans distrust concepts like the International Criminal Court and claims by the UN to be the "sole source of legitimacy" for the use of force, because Americans have a profound distrust of accumulated power. Our Founding Fathers created a government founded on a system of checks and balances and on dispersal of power.

In his 1962 classic, *Capitalism and Freedom*, the Nobel prize-winning economist Milton Friedman rightly declared: "[G]overnment power must be dispersed. If government is to exercise power, better in the county than in the state, better in the state than in Washington. [Because] if I do not like what my local community does, I can move to another local community...[and] if I do not like what my state does, I can move to another. [But] if I do not like what Washington imposes, I have few alternatives in this world of jealous nations."

Forty years later, as the UN seeks to impose its utopian vision of "international law" on Americans, we can add this question: Where do we go when we don't like the "laws" of the world?

Today, while our friends in Europe concede more and more power upwards to supranational institutions like the European Union, Americans are heading in precisely the opposite direction.

America is in a process of reducing centralized power by taking more and more authority that had been amassed by the federal government in Washington and referring it to the individual states, where it rightly belongs.

This is why Americans reject the idea of a sovereign United Nations that presumes to be the source of legitimacy for the United States government's policies, foreign or domestic. There is only one source of legitimacy of the American government's policies—and that is the consent of the American people.

If the United Nations is to survive into the twenty-first century, it must recognize its limitations. The demands of the United States have not changed much since Henry Cabot Lodge laid out his conditions for joining the League of Nations eighty years ago: Americans want to ensure that the United States of America remains the sole judge of its own internal affairs, that the United Nations is not allowed to restrict the individual rights of U.S. citizens, and that the United States retains sole authority over the deployment of U.S. forces around the world.

This is what Americans ask of the United Nations; it is what Americans expect of the United Nations. A United Nations that focuses on helping sovereign states work together is worth keeping; a United Nations that insists on trying to impose a utopian vision on America and the world will collapse under its own weight.

If the United Nations respects the sovereign rights of the American people and serves them as an effective tool of diplomacy, it will earn and deserve their respect and support. But a United Nations that seeks to impose its presumed authority on the American people without their consent begs for confrontation and, I want to be candid, eventual U.S. withdrawal.

Thank you very much.

A WELCOME TO WASHINGTON
A Greeting to the United Nations Security Council on Its Visit to the Old Senate Chamber, Washington, D.C., March 30, 2000

DISTINGUISHED AMBASSADORS, Dr. Baker, Ladies and Gentlemen, on behalf of the Foreign Relations Committee—and, indeed, on behalf of all ninety-nine of my Senate colleagues—it is my great pleasure to welcome you to the United States Senate.

My colleagues and I very much appreciated the warm welcome you all extended to us during our visit to the United Nations in January, and we are grateful to have the opportunity today not only to repay your hospitality but especially to continue the important dialogue we began in New York.

We welcome you this morning in a room filled with history. The United States Senate met in this chamber from 1810 until 1859—except for a brief period in 1814 after the British marched on Washington and set fire to the Capitol Building. (No need to worry, Ambassador Greenstock, we got over it a long time ago.)

It was in this chamber that the "Great Triumvirate" of senators—Daniel Webster, Henry Clay, and John C. Calhoun—conducted some of the greatest debates in our nation's history, during what was known as the Senate's "golden age." And, after the Senate left for larger quarters, this chamber is where the United States Supreme Court deliberated until 1935.

Now, with your groundbreaking visit to the United States Senate, we are adding another chapter to the illustrious history of this room.

It is indeed appropriate that you have begun your visit today in this chamber. For in this room, two of the three coequal branches of our nation's government held some of their greatest deliberations.

This is significant because, for many of our friends from foreign lands, our tripartite system of government is a mysterious institution. I know it has been suggested to you that the president alone speaks for the United States in foreign affairs. And in most nations of the world—even the great democracies—that is indeed the case; the executive branch of government dominates, indeed has a near monopoly in, the conduct of foreign policy.

Not so the United States. Our Founding Fathers had a brilliant and revolutionary vision in establishing the separation of powers, a government with three independent and coequal branches—the executive branch, the Congress, and the judicial branch. For those coming from countries with different systems, it is sometimes difficult for visitors to appreciate the unique role the United States Senate plays in setting our nation's foreign policy agenda.

The United States can enter into no treaty without the advice and consent of the Senate (some presidents have gotten into trouble by demanding the Senate's consent while spurning the Senate's advice); no ambassador can represent this nation abroad without the Senate's approval; and no foreign policy initiative that involves the taxpayers' money can go forward without those funds being authorized by Congress (as you are no doubt aware).

When I had the privilege of addressing you in New York, I said to you that if we are to have a new beginning in U.S.-UN relations, we must endeavor to understand each other better. In my meetings with the distinguished secretary-general and his staff—and in visiting with you at the UN—I learned a great deal about that institution.

To reciprocate, I have asked the director of the Senate Historical Office, Richard Baker, to come here this morning and share with you some of the history of the U.S. Senate—the world's greatest deliberative body—and its role in the making of U.S. foreign policy. It is my hope that this will be helpful to you and give you a better understanding of this institution, the U.S. Senate.

With the Foreign Relations Committee's visit to New York, and now with your visit here today, I think we can say—quite literally—that we are making history together. I hope that we can continue to do so.

Chapter 4
NATO—An Alliance That Works

SENATOR HELMS IS HIGHLY SKEPTICAL of most international institutions. But one institution that works is the NATO alliance. NATO works because of American leadership and because it has maintained a limited mission: the territorial defense of its member countries. Which is why Senator Helms led the fight for NATO expansion—and against NATO transformation.

The following two essays represent the "bookends" of that debate.

The first appeared in European editions of the *Wall Street Journal* just as NATO leaders were gathering in Madrid to formally invite Poland, Hungary, and the Czech Republic to join the alliance. Senator Helms expressed his support for the expansion but warned that the Clinton administration was endangering the chances for Senate approval of that expansion with its plans to transform NATO.

He listed ten conditions that the president would have to meet before the Foreign Relations Committee would consider approving the expansion protocols. The same day the essay appeared, a call came from the president's plane (en route from Madrid to Warsaw) with a message for the chairman—the president and Secretary of State Madeleine Albright had read the essay and would work to meet his conditions.

Over the next several months, the Foreign Relations Committee and the administration worked out each of the conditions in a series of hearings. By the time the expansion protocols reached the Senate floor, the debate went so smoothly that many in the media complained that the Senate was not having a serious debate on this momentous decision. The fact is, they had missed the debate—it had taken place inside the Foreign Relations Committee months before. In the second essay, published just as the Senate prepared to vote, Senator Helms laid out all the issues that had been resolved and urged his colleagues to vote yes.

These two essays show how Senator Helms championed both the cause of NATO expansion and the concerns of NATO expansion's critics. By keeping a foot in each camp and resolving each of the key issues ahead of time, he was able to ensure that by the time the treaty reached the full Senate, the foes of expansion were left with no issues around which to rally opposition.

As a result, NATO expansion was done . . . and done the right way.

NEW MEMBERS, NOT NEW MISSIONS
Wall Street Journal Europe, July 9, 1997

As NATO LEADERS MEET IN MADRID to discuss the enlargement of the alliance, some words of caution are in order. The Clinton administration's egregious mishandling of NATO expansion is raising serious concerns in the U.S. Senate, which must approve any enlargement treaty.

There is growing distress among supporters of enlargement (like myself) that the administration's plan for NATO expansion may be evolving into a dangerous and ill-considered plan for NATO transformation, that we are inviting new nations not into the NATO that won the Cold War but rather into a new, diluted NATO, converted from a well-defined military alliance into a nebulous "collective security" arrangement.

To date, the Clinton administration has failed to present the Senate with any credible strategic rationale for NATO expansion—that is, no explanation of the threat posed to the Atlantic alliance, nor why an expanded NATO is needed to counter it.

Instead, all sorts of misguided proposals are floating around for transforming NATO's mission and purpose in an effort to justify alliance expansion.

Deputy Secretary of State Strobe Talbott, the Clinton administration's point man on NATO expansion, argues that while "during the Cold War, military and geopolitical considerations mainly determined NATO's decisions . . . today, with the end of the Cold War, nonmilitary goals can and should help shape the new NATO." NATO's primary mission, Mr. Talbott is saying, should no longer be the defense of Europe but rather "promoting democracy within NATO states and good relations among them"—in other words, nation building.

Others see this "new NATO" serving as a stand-in peacekeeper for a United Nations discredited by its failures in Somalia and Bosnia. Indeed, the NATO-Russia "Founding Act," largely negotiated by the Clinton administration, enshrines this new role for NATO, hailing NATO's historic transformation in making "new missions of peacekeeping and crisis management in support of the UN" primary alliance functions.

Advocates of NATO transformation make a better case for the alliance to disband than expand. NATO's job is not to replace the UN as the world's peacekeeper, nor is it to build democracy and pan-European harmony or promote better relations with Russia. NATO has proven the most successful military alliance in history precisely because it has rejected utopian temptations to remake the world.

Rather, NATO's mission today must be the same clear-cut and limited mission it undertook at its inception: to protect the territorial integrity of its members, defend them from external aggression, and prevent the hegemony of any one state in Europe.

The state that sought hegemony during the latter half of this century was Russia. The state most likely to seek hegemony in the beginning of the next century is also Russia. A central strategic rationale for expanding NATO must be to hedge against the possible return of a nationalist or imperialist Russia, with twenty thousand nuclear missiles and ambitions of restoring its lost empire. NATO enlargement, as Henry Kissinger argues, must be undertaken to "encourage Russian leaders to interrupt the fateful rhythm of Russian history... and discourage Russia's historical policy of creating a security belt of important and, if possible, politically dependent states around its borders."

Unfortunately, the Clinton administration does not see this as a legitimate strategic rationale for expansion. "Fear of a new wave of Russian imperialism ... should not be seen as the driving force behind NATO enlargement," says Mr. Talbott.

Not surprisingly, those states seeking NATO membership seem to understand NATO's purpose better than the alliance leader. Lithuania's former president, Vytautas Landsbergis, put it bluntly: "We are an endangered country. We are calling for protection." Poland, which spent much of its history under one form or another of Russian occupation, makes clear that it seeks NATO membership as a guarantee of its territorial integrity. And when Czech president Vaclav Havel warned of "another Munich," he was calling on us not to leave Central Europe once again at the mercy of any great power, as Neville Chamberlain did in 1938. Poland, Hungary, the Czech Republic, and other potential candidate states don't need NATO to establish democracy. They need NATO to protect the democracies they have already established from external aggression.

Sadly, Mr. Havel's admonishments not to appease "chauvinistic, Great Russian, crypto-communist, and crypto-totalitarian forces" have been largely ignored by the Clinton administration. Quite the opposite: The administration has turned NATO expansion into an exercise in the appeasement of Russia.

After admitting East Germany in 1990 (and giving the Soviet Union neither a "voice" nor a "veto" in the process), the United States delayed NATO expansion for nearly seven years in a misguided effort to secure Russian approval. Russia, knowing an opportunity when it sees one, has used its opposition to NATO expansion to gain all sorts of concessions, ranging from arms control capitulations to the NATO-Russia "Founding Act."

That agreement concedes "primary responsibility... for international peace and security" to the UN Security Council, where Russia has a veto. It gives Russia (the very country NATO is constituted to deter) a voice at every level of the alliance's deliberations. And it gives Russia a seat at the table before any candidate members (those being brought in to protect them from aggression) get a seat at the table.

It is my sincere hope that the U.S. Senate can approve NATO expansion. But if we are to do so, some dramatic changes must be made. As chairman of the Senate committee that must approve the resolution of ratification, I urge the administration to take the following steps before presenting NATO expansion to the Senate:

- Outline a clear, complete strategic security rationale for NATO expansion.

- Agree that no limitation will be placed on the numbers of NATO troops or types of weapons to be deployed on territory of new member states (including tactical nuclear weapons)— there must be no second-class citizens in NATO.

- Explicitly reject Russian efforts to establish a "nuclear weapons–free zone" in Central Europe.

- Explicitly reject all efforts to tie NATO decisions to UN Security Council approval.

- Establish a clear delineation of NATO deliberations that are off-limits to Russia (including, but not limited to, arms control, further alliance expansion, procurement, and strategic doctrine).

- Provide an immediate seat at the NATO table for countries invited to join the alliance.

- Reject Russian efforts to require NATO aid for Russian arms sales to former Warsaw Pact militaries joining the alliance, as a quid pro quo for NATO expansion—NATO must not become a back channel for new foreign aid to Russia.

- Reject any further Russian efforts to link concessions in arms control negotiations—including the antiquated ABM Treaty and the Conventional Forces in Europe (CFE) Treaty—to NATO expansion.

- Develop a plan for a NATO ballistic missile defense system to defend Europe.

- Get clear advance agreement on an equitable distribution of the cost of expansion, to make certain that American taxpayers don't get stuck with the lion's share of the bill.

Is renewed Russian aggression the only strategic threat NATO must consider? Of course not. There are many potential threats to Europe, including the possibility of rogue states like Libya and Iran one day threatening the continent with weapons of mass destruction. But the Clinton administration has failed to define NATO expansion in terms of any strategic threat.

If the Clinton administration views NATO not as a tool to defend Europe but as a laboratory for social work, then NATO should not only eschew expansion, it should declare victory and close shop. The costs of maintaining NATO, much less expanding it, cannot be justified if its mission is democracy building and peacekeeping. There are other, less expensive and more appropriate forums for such ventures (such as the European Union and the Organization for Security and Cooperation in Europe). NATO is a military alliance—it must remain so or go out of business.

NATO EXPANSION HAS ALL THE SAFEGUARDS IT NEEDS
Wall Street Journal, **March 23, 1998**

NINE MONTHS AGO I issued a warning to the Clinton administration: Its mishandling of NATO expansion was endangering chances for Senate ratification. Many senators (who in principle supported bringing the Czech Republic, Hungary, and Poland into the North Atlantic Treaty Organization) were greatly concerned that the administration's plan was evolving into a dangerous and ill-considered plan for NATO transformation.

At the time, the administration had not presented the Senate with a strategic rationale for NATO expansion. Quite the opposite: Deputy Secretary of State Strobe Talbott was arguing that with the end of the Cold War, "military and geopolitical considerations should take a back seat as 'other nonmilitary goals' ... shape the new NATO." Worse still was the administration's effort to appease Moscow by giving Russia a "voice" in NATO decision making. All this, I sought to warn the administration, was not going to fly on Capitol Hill.

During the next nine months, I worked closely with Secretary of State Madeleine Albright to make a number of important course corrections. As the Senate prepares to vote on NATO expansion, I can report with confidence that we have successfully addressed the major areas of concern.

The administration has agreed to a tightly worded Resolution of Ratification, which includes strict, legally binding language that:

- Requires that "the core purpose of NATO must continue to be the collective defense of the territory of all NATO members"—not peacekeeping or "nonmilitary" goals.

- Requires NATO defense planning, command structures, and force goals to be centered on ensuring the territorial defense of member countries.

- Ensures that Russia will have neither a voice nor a veto in NATO decision making, and that the NATO-Russian "Permanent Joint Council" will be a forum for explaining—not negotiating—NATO policy.

- Requires extensive consultation with the Senate in the case of any proposed changes in the strategic concept of NATO.

- Reaffirms that NATO does not require the consent of the United Nations, or any other international organization, to take action to defend its members' security.

- Requires the administration to report to Congress on a plan for a NATO ballistic missile defense system to protect Europe.

- Places strict limits on the cost to U.S. taxpayers for expansion.

Had the administration refused to accept these and other conditions, I would be on the Senate floor leading the fight to delay NATO expansion.

Still, some of my Senate colleagues are concerned about the potential "dilution" of NATO. I share this concern. But we must be clear: The act of adding these new members will not dilute NATO. What we must prevent is the dilution of NATO's mission and purpose by ensuring that peacekeeping and nation building do not eclipse territorial defense as primary alliance functions.

If anything, adding the Czech Republic, Hungary, and Poland to NATO will help stop such a dilution of the alliance's core mission. These nations—all of which spent much of this century under foreign occupation or control—understand better than anyone the need to focus on territorial defense. To prevent NATO dilution, the Foreign Relations Committee has taken explicit steps to require that NATO defense planning remain focused on territorial defense and tied to the security of NATO members (rather than vague concepts like European "stability").

That said, it would be unwise for the Senate explicitly to restrict NATO's ability to act "out of area." Consider: The day may not be far off when the principal threat to the territory of NATO members will be not a resurgent Russia but a missile strike or terrorist attack by a rogue state such as Iran, Iraq, Libya, Syria, or even North Korea. Would we really want to constrain NATO's ability to respond against a regime that dared to use chemical or biological weapons on the territory of a NATO member? Would we want to bar NATO's ability to strike "out of area" to prevent such an attack? Of course not.

Another concern is that NATO expansion could somehow derail Russia's democratic experiment. But this argument is dead wrong. NATO is a defensive alliance of democratic nations with no hostile intentions toward Russia. NATO expansion in no way threatens Russian democracy or precludes friendly relations with Russia. If anything, expanding the alliance will make constructive relations with Russia easier because a stronger NATO will shut off Russia's avenues to destructive patterns of behavior.

Others have suggested the Senate demand that aspiring NATO members first gain admission to the European Union. This would be nothing less than the abdication of U.S. leadership in Europe. It would be ludicrous to give a veto over NATO to the EU—which may keep these countries out in order to protect its own agricultural markets from competition. Since when do we allow French farmers to decide what is in America's security interests?

The Czech Republic, Hungary, and Poland will be among the most reliable, pro-American NATO allies we could hope for. Not only do these countries need NATO, but the United States needs these countries in NATO. They will be among the first to stand with us in times of crisis and will support America as we work to ensure that NATO remains what it is today—the most effective military alliance in human history. We have, through the efforts of many senators, ensured that NATO expansion is done the right way. Now is the time to act.

Chapter 5

The Arms Control Heresy

IN SENATOR HELMS'S VIEW, U.S. security policy has for years been held hostage by a dangerous cult—one that worships at the altar of arms control.

This cult's greatest accomplishment has been its success in preventing the development of a national missile defense, thanks to the antiquated 1972 ABM Treaty, which bars the United States from deploying such defenses.

In 1983 President Reagan announced America's intention to build and deploy defenses to protect the United States from ballistic missile attack. Seventeen years later, at the dawn of a new century, that goal remains unachieved.

However, a watershed event took place in October 1999, when the U.S. Senate voted for the first time in its history to reject a major arms control agreement—the Comprehensive Test Ban Treaty (CTBT). As Senator Helms notes below, condemnation rang out from across the globe with the Senate's defeat of this pact. But with the CTBT's defeat, a Rubicon was crossed.

In these essays, Senator Helms describes the reasons for the defeat of the CTBT and responds to the widespread hysteria in Europe over the Senate's historic vote. He further explains why the time has come—finally—to get rid of the antiquated ABM Treaty and also describes his earlier, uphill battle against the Chemical Weapons Convention—a treaty Helms likened to the Kellogg-Briand pact of the 1920s, which "banned" war (it sounded good in theory, but in practice it would not, and could not, accomplish its desired goal).

~~~~~~~~

COMMITTING TO MISSILE DEFENSE
Izvestia, June 5, 2000

PRESIDENT CLINTON WANTS, in his final months in office, to strike a major arms control deal with Russia, including a new ABM Treaty that would limit the United States' ability to defend itself against ballistic missile attack.

White House officials have openly stated their concern that Mr. Clinton faces the prospect of leaving office without a major arms control agreement to his credit—the first president in memory to do so.

So Mr. Clinton wants an agreement, a signing ceremony, a picture of him shaking hands with President Putin, broad smiles on their faces, with large, ornately bound treaties under their arms, as the cameras click for perhaps the last time—a final curtain call of sorts.

If the price of that final curtain call is a resurrection of the defunct U.S.-Soviet ABM Treaty that would prevent the United States from protecting itself against missile attack, then that price is far too high.

For nearly eight years, while North Korea and Iran raced forward with their nuclear programs, and while China stole the most advanced nuclear secrets of the United States, and while Iraq escaped international inspections, President Clinton did everything in his power to stand in the way of deploying a national missile defense.

Within three years of taking office, Mr. Clinton had completely gutted the U.S. national missile defense program, slashing the national missile defense budget by more than 80 percent. In 1997 he signed two agreements to revive and expand the U.S.-Soviet

ABM Treaty (then, heeding some of his advisors, refused to honor his legal commitment to submit those agreements to the U.S. Senate, for fear that the Senate would reject them). Mr. Clinton repeatedly blocked enactment of missile defense legislation approved by Congress and grudgingly signed a missile defense law in 1999—but only after it passed both houses of Congress by a veto-proof majority, and only after the independent Rumsfeld Commission had issued a stinging, bipartisan report declaring that the Clinton administration had dramatically underestimated the ballistic missile threat to the United States.

But while Mr. Clinton was doing all this—costing the United States almost eight years in a race against time to deploy missile defenses—our adversaries were forging ahead with their missile systems.

While Mr. Clinton was dragging his feet, foreign ballistic missile threats to the United States grew in terms of both range and sophistication. Today, several third world nations possess, or are developing, ballistic missiles capable of delivering chemical, biological, or nuclear warheads against U.S. cities.

According to the Rumsfeld Commission, both North Korea and Iran are within five years of possessing viable ICBMs capable of striking the continental United States—and North Korea may already (today) have the capacity to strike Alaska and Hawaii. And just last month, Communist China explicitly threatened to use nuclear weapons against U.S. cities should the United States take any action to defend democratic Taiwan in the event that Beijing launched an invasion.

But now, in the twilight of his presidency, Mr. Clinton wants to strike an ill-considered deal to purchase Russian consent to an inadequate U.S. missile defense—one single site in Alaska, to be deployed, but not until 2005—in exchange for a new, revitalized

ABM Treaty that would permanently ban any truly national missile defense.

The president is attempting to lock the United States into a system that cannot defend the American people against even the limited threats we face today. And the president is trying to resurrect the U.S.-Soviet ABM Treaty to make impossible any future enhancements to national missile defense.

The agreement Mr. Clinton proposes would not permit spaced-based sensors; it would not permit sufficient numbers of ground-based radars; and it would not permit additional defenses based on alternate missile interceptor systems—such as naval sea-based interceptors. All of these, and more, are necessary to achieve a fully effective defense against the full range of possible threats.

Mr. Clinton's proposal is not a plan to defend the United States; it is a plan to leave the United States defenseless. It is, in fact, a plan to salvage the antiquated and invalid U.S.-Soviet ABM Treaty.

It is a plan that is going nowhere fast.

After dragging his feet on missile defense for nearly eight years, Mr. Clinton now fervently hopes that he will be permitted, in his final months in office, to tie the hands of the next president.

Well I, for one, have a message for the president: Not on my watch.

Let's be clear, to avoid any misunderstandings: Any modified ABM Treaty negotiated by this administration will be dead on arrival at the Senate Foreign Relations Committee.

In a few months, the American people will go to the polls to elect a new president—a president that must make a clean break from the failed policies of this administration.

It is my intent to do everything in my power to ensure that nothing is done in the next few months, by this administration, to tie the hands of the next administration in pursuing a new national security policy—a policy based not on scraps of parchment but rather on concrete defenses; a policy designed to protect the American people from ballistic missile attack; a policy designed to ensure that no hostile regime—from Tehran to Pyongyang to Beijing—is capable of threatening the United States of America with nuclear blackmail.

The decision on missile defense will be for the next president to make.

For this administration—after opposing missile defense for eight years—to attempt at the eleventh hour to try to negotiate a revised ABM Treaty is too little, too late. This administration has long had its chance to adopt a new security approach to meet the new threats and challenges of the post–Cold War era. The administration chose not to do so.

Now, this administration's time for grand treaty initiatives is at an end. For the remainder of this year, the Foreign Relations Committee will continue its routine work—we will consider tax treaties, extradition treaties, and other already negotiated treaties. But we will not consider any new, last-minute arms control measures that this administration negotiates in its final, closing months in office.

And, as chairman of this committee, I should make it clear that the Foreign Relations Committee will not consider the next administration bound by any treaties this administration may try to negotiate in the coming months.

The Russian government should not be under any illusion whatsoever that any commitments made by this lame-duck administration will be binding on the next administration.

America has waited eight years for a commitment to build and deploy a national missile defense. We can wait a few more months for a president committed to doing it and doing it right—to protect the American people.

WHY THE SENATE SAID NO TO THE
NUCLEAR TEST BAN TREATY
Wall Street Journal, October 18, 1999

SINCE THE SENATE VOTED OVERWHELMINGLY to reject the Comprehensive Test Ban Treaty (CTBT), condemnation bordering on hysteria has rung out from the capitals of the world.

Italy's foreign minister accused the Senate of "halting the process...of achieving complete global nuclear disarmament" (to which I plead nolo contendere). German foreign minister Joschka Fischer declared the vote "a serious setback for nuclear nonproliferation." And French president Jacques Chirac (who, with his German and British counterparts, penned a *New York Times* op-ed before the vote lecturing the Senate on its responsibility to ratify the test ban) declared that by rejecting his advice the Senate had launched "an attack on the process of nonproliferation and disarmament, which is one of the priorities of the European Union."

With all due respect to Mr. Chirac, the last time I checked, no nation was counting on the safety and reliability of the French nuclear arsenal to guarantee its security. Many do, however, depend on the United States for nuclear guarantees.

The Senate rejected the CTBT—but not to score political points against a lame-duck administration, and certainly not because we are in the grip of "neoisolationism," as President Clinton deliriously suggested. The Senate rejected the CTBT because it was a dangerous and unverifiable treaty that would have endangered the safety and reliability of the U.S. nuclear arsenal and undermined U.S. security and the security of our allies.

Our European friends fail to understand that the United States has unique responsibilities in the world. Unlike smaller powers, America is not free to ratify fanciful treaties like the CTBT (or, for that matter, the Ottawa Land Mines Convention or the International Criminal Court), which do no good but restrict our ability to meet our international commitments.

That is why treaty supporters' Chicken Little arguments swayed few if any senators. The Senate was warned that if we voted down the CTBT, India and Pakistan may well proceed with nuclear tests. Well, I have news for them: India and Pakistan have already tested. Why? Because of the Clinton administration's failed nuclear nonproliferation policies.

For years, India's leaders watched as China transferred M-11 missiles to Pakistan and the Clinton administration refused to impose sanctions on China that are required by law. India understandably concluded that the president of the United States is not serious about nonproliferation and that this White House is unwilling to impose a real cost on proliferating nations.

This administration, in its shameful effort to curry favor with Silicon Valley executives, has loosened export controls on supercomputers, putting them in Russian nuclear weapons factories. The administration has decontrolled satellite launches, helping China improve its nuclear missile force. The administration has looked the other way as Russia has been repeatedly caught assisting both Iran and Iraq in their drive to build weapons of mass destruction.

As long as such negligence continues, rogue nations will continue to develop those weapons, Russia and China will continue clandestine nuclear testing, North Korea will continue to blackmail the West with its nuclear program, and India and Pakistan will probably test again. They will do it not because the Senate rejected the CTBT but because the administration is unwilling to impose any real costs.

By defeating this treaty, the Senate did not, as Mr. Clinton angrily suggests, give a "green light" for nuclear testing. Tests by nonnuclear states are already a violation of the international norm established by the Nuclear Nonproliferation Treaty. Only by showing a willingness to impose real penalties on such violations will we ever prevent the expansion of the nuclear club. Papering over the problem with a worthless treaty accomplishes nothing.

Let me suggest one good thing that will happen now that the CTBT has been defeated: This administration, and future administrations, will think twice before signing bad treaties that cannot pass muster in the Senate. Mr. Clinton clearly wants the Senate's "consent" on its treaties, but he is unwilling to take our "advice." If he had sought our advice before signing the CTBT, it would have been clear well in advance that an unverifiable, permanent, zero-yield ban on all nuclear tests would be defeated.

The Senate had no choice but to reject the CTBT explicitly and unquestionably. Had we postponed the vote, under customary international law the United States, as a signatory nation, would have been bound by the CTBT's terms. We had to vote to make clear that the United States will not be legally bound by the terms of this treaty.

We had to vote for another reason as well: to make certain that the next administration will be left free to establish its own nuclear nonproliferation policies, unencumbered by the failed policies of its predecessor. The new president must have a free hand to reestablish American credibility on nonproliferation matters—credibility based not on scraps of paper but on clear resolve, a credible nuclear deterrent, and real defenses against ballistic missile attack.

The Senate had a solemn responsibility to vote on—and to reject—the Comprehensive Test Ban Treaty. We did it not for politics but for our national security. If that does not please Mr. Chirac and company, *c'est la vie.*

AMEND THE ABM TREATY? NO, SCRAP IT
Wall Street Journal, **January 22, 1999**

UNDER PRESSURE FROM THE PENTAGON and congressional conservatives, President Clinton reluctantly decided to request $6.6 billion over six years in his new budget for missile defense research. And Defense Secretary William Cohen announced yesterday that the administration wants permission from Russia to renegotiate the Anti-Ballistic Missile (ABM) Treaty.

But administration officials have made it clear that unless the Russians are willing to give that permission, they have no intention of actually deploying a nationwide missile defense system. Why? Because the administration believes that any such deployment would violate the ABM Treaty. And, as National Security Advisor Samuel Berger affirmed in a speech just last week, "We remain strongly committed to the 1972 Anti-Ballistic Missile Treaty [as] a cornerstone to our security."

What that means is that in Mr. Berger's view, deploying even the most limited missile defense would require getting permission from Russia to revise the ABM Treaty. Consider that for a moment: The Clinton administration wants to negotiate permission from Russia over whether the United States can protect itself from ballistic missile attack by North Korea.

The ABM Treaty is the root of our problems. So long as it is a "cornerstone" of U.S. security policy, as Mr. Berger says, we will never be able to deploy a nationwide missile defense that will provide real security for the American people.

We do not need to renegotiate the ABM Treaty to build and deploy national missile defense. We can do it today. The ABM Treaty is dead. It died when our treaty partner, the Soviet Union, ceased to exist. But rather than move swiftly to declare the treaty dead, and build and deploy a national missile defense, the Clinton administration is attempting to resuscitate the ABM Treaty with new protocols to apply its terms to Russia and all the other nuclear states that were once part of the Soviet Union.

The world has changed a great deal since the ABM Treaty was first ratified twenty-seven years ago. The United States faces new and very different threats today—threats that are growing daily. China has nineteen intercontinental ballistic missiles, thirteen of which are aimed at the United States. As recently as 1997 a senior Chinese official issued a veiled nuclear threat, warning that the United States would never come to the defense of Taiwan because we Americans "care more about Los Angeles than Taipei."

Saddam Hussein is doggedly pursuing nuclear, chemical, and biological weapons and the long-range missiles to deliver them, and the will of the international community to confront and disarm him is crumbling. Iran, which is also developing a nuclear capability, just tested a new missile—built with Russian, Chinese, and North Korean technology—which can strike Israel and Turkey, a NATO ally. And according to the Rumsfeld Commission, Iran "has acquired and is seeking advanced missile components that can be combined to produce ballistic missiles with sufficient range to strike the United States." If Iran succeeds, the commission warns, it will be capable of striking all the way to St. Paul, Minnesota.

North Korea's unstable communist regime is forging ahead with its nuclear weapons program and test-fired a missile over Japan last August that is capable of striking both Alaska and Hawaii. And Pyongyang is close to testing a new missile, the TD-2, which could allow it to strike the continental United States.

Today America is vulnerable to ballistic missile attack by unstable outlaw regimes, and that missile threat will increase dramatically in the early years of the twenty-first century. What are we doing today, in this waning year of the twentieth century, to defend ourselves against these emerging threats? Practically nothing.

When the Senate votes on the new protocols expanding the ABM Treaty to Russia and other post-Soviet states, we will in fact be voting on the ABM Treaty itself. For the first time in twenty-seven years, the Senate will have a chance to reexamine the wisdom of that dangerous treaty. If I succeed, we will defeat the ABM Treaty, toss it into the dustbin of history, and thereby clear the way to build a national missile defense.

The Clinton administration wants to avoid that at all costs. So the president has delayed sending the new protocols to the Senate for approval. But Mr. Clinton does not have a choice—he is required by law to submit the ABM protocols to the Senate. On May 14, 1997, Mr. Clinton agreed to explicit, legally binding language that he submit the protocols, a condition that I required during the ratification of another treaty, the Conventional Forces in Europe Flank Document. It has been 618 days since Mr. Clinton made that commitment under law. I am going to hold him to it.

Today I am setting a deadline for the president to submit the ABM protocols to the Senate. I expect them to arrive by June 1. In the meantime, I will begin ratification hearings on the treaty shortly so that the Foreign Relations Committee will be ready to vote and report the treaty to the full Senate by June 1. I say to the president: Let your administration make its case for the ABM Treaty, we will make our case against it, and let the Senate vote. If I have my way, the Senate this year will clear the way for the deployment of national missile defense.

Not until the administration has submitted the ABM protocols and the Kyoto global-warming treaty, and the Senate has completed its consideration of them, will the Foreign Relations Committee turn its attention to other treaties on the president's agenda.

Mr. Clinton cannot demand quick action on treaties he wants us to consider and at the same time hold hostage other treaties he is afraid we will reject. The president must submit all of them, or we will consider none of them.

CLINTON'S TOOTHLESS
NONPROLIFERATION POLICY
Wall Street Journal, June 18, 1998

FACING THE COLLAPSE OF HIS NONPROLIFERATION POLICY and the emergence of India and Pakistan as declared nuclear powers, President Clinton is touting a toothless arms control pact as a panacea. After ten nuclear tests by India and Pakistan, Mr. Clinton is pushing these countries to sign the Comprehensive Test Ban Treaty (CTBT) and is demanding quick Senate ratification of the accord.

Getting India and Pakistan to sign the CTBT now would amount to nothing more than closing the stable door after the horses have galloped away. What earthly good is a "test ban" if nations join the treaty only after carrying out all their planned tests? Besides, the CTBT is a dead letter for the foreseeable future. The treaty itself states that it cannot take effect until forty-four specific nations (including not only India and Pakistan but also North Korea and Iran) ratify the pact. That's not going to happen anytime soon.

The administration needs to face some facts: The nuclear club is expanding; China and Russia are recklessly proliferating danger-ous technology to rogue regimes; and some two dozen nations, many of them hostile to the United States, are working to develop nuclear, chemical, and biological weapons and the missile technology to deliver them. The threat of ballistic missile attack on the United States is growing rapidly—and, incredible as it may seem, the United States cannot stop a ballistic missile headed for an American city.

What is needed now is not another meaningless arms control treaty like the CTBT. What is needed is a credible nonprolifera-tion policy and a national missile defense to protect the United States against the growing threat of nuclear, chemical, and bio-logical weapons attack. For more than twenty-five years the impediment to building such a defense has been the 1972 Anti-Ballistic Missile Treaty, in which the Soviet Union and the United States agreed not to defend themselves from missile attack.

Today, with the collapse of our treaty partner, the ABM Treaty is defunct. But instead of moving ahead with a national missile defense to protect the American people, Mr. Clinton wants to revive the ABM Treaty and its restrictions on missile defense. He has negotiated protocols that would not only revive the treaty but also expand it to include new countries that did not even exist when the original ABM Treaty was ratified. These protocols would make missile defense for the United States impossible.

The Senate is poised to vote this year on Mr. Clinton's ABM protocols—but he is refusing to allow the vote to take place. Even as Mr. Clinton is pushing for quick Senate action on the discredited CTBT, he is holding the ABM protocols hostage, refusing to submit them for the Senate's advice and consent.

The vote on the ABM protocols would be the first time in the twenty-six years since the ABM Treaty was ratified that the Senate has had a chance to reexamine the wisdom of that dangerous pact. The administration is desperate to prevent such a reconsideration. The president fears that, given the strong support in Congress for national missile defense, the Senate may actually reject the ABM protocols—and that such a defeat would be a devastating rejection of the ABM Treaty itself.

Mr. Clinton's fears may well be justified: I will be leading the charge to defeat the ABM protocols and to clear the way for national missile defense. But the president cannot pick which treaties the Senate will consider and which ones it will not. Submitting the ABM protocols to the Senate is not a matter of discretion for Mr. Clinton—it is a matter of law. And Mr. Clinton should not expect swift action on a treaty he wants the Senate to vote on while at the same time holding hostage other treaties on which he does not want a Senate vote.

In addition to his constitutional obligations, on May 15, 1997, he entered into an agreement with the Senate requiring, in explicit, legally binding language, that he submit the ABM protocols to the Senate. This is a condition I required during the ratification of the Conventional Forces in Europe Flank Document. After more than a year and numerous requests from the Senate, the president has still failed to release the ABM protocols.

We cannot afford to wait any longer. The world has changed a great deal since the ABM Treaty was ratified in the midst of the Cold War. The danger posed by rogue states possessing weapons of mass destruction is growing, and with it the need for a robust ballistic missile defense. The time has come for the Senate to conduct a thorough review of this antiquated treaty and decide whether the United States should be bound by it in a world of rapidly proliferating threats.

I intend to begin Foreign Relations Committee consideration of the ABM protocols shortly and to have a full Senate vote on them before Congress adjourns this year. Only the continued intransigence of the Clinton administration could prevent such a vote.

Such intransigence would have consequences for the administration. If the White House expects cooperation from the Senate on its priorities, then I expect to have its full cooperation with the committee's consideration of the ABM protocols. It is unacceptable for the administration to hold these agreements (as well as other accords, such as the Kyoto Protocol on Global Climate Change) hostage simply because it believes they might be rejected by the Senate.

Instead of pushing a new treaty that papers over India's and Pakistan's nuclear tests, the administration must require them to roll back their nuclear ban—the Nuclear Nonproliferation Treaty—which already has 185 signatories and has been in force since 1970.

Waving around the worthless CTBT is no substitute for a competent nonproliferation policy. It is no substitute for punishing China's proliferation activities. And it is certainly no substitute for national missile defense.

Let the president make his case for reviving the ABM Treaty. We who support deployment of national missile defense will make ours. But the Senate must vote on the ABM protocols and the fate of the ABM Treaty this year.

A TREATY THAT'S WORSE THAN NOTHING
Washington Post, April 23, 1997

THERE ARE AMPLE REASONS for the U.S. Senate to reject the Chemical Weapons Convention (CWC): the fact that the treaty won't touch terrorist states such as Libya, Iraq, Syria, and North Korea; the administration's admission that the treaty is unverifiable; Russia's cheating on it even before the convention goes into effect; and the administration's incredible refusal to bar inspectors from hostile nations such as Iran and China. Each of these defects in and of itself is reason enough to oppose the treaty.

But the one issue that has raised the greatest concern among senators—the issue on which the ratification vote will almost certainly hinge—is the Clinton administration's refusal to modify the treaty's Articles 10 and 11.

These controversial provisions require the transfer of dangerous chemical agents, defensive gear, and know-how to any nation that joins the CWC—including terrorist states such as Iran and Cuba and known proliferators such as Russia and China. Articles 10 and 11, former defense secretary Dick Cheney told the Senate Foreign Relations Committee earlier this month, "amount to a formula for greatly accelerating the proliferation of chemical warfare capabilities around the world."

Senate majority leader Trent Lott and I have inserted a protection in the Senate's resolution of ratification that would make approval of the treaty absolutely contingent on the administration's agreement to seek modifications of Articles 10 and 11. The administration must now decide whether it will try to strip out that key protection. If it insists that the Senate vote on the treaty with Articles 10 and 11 left intact, it will be inviting the Senate to reject the treaty entirely—and the Senate should do so.

Why is modification of Articles 10 and 11 so vital? The Clinton administration argues that, despite all its flaws, the CWC is "better than nothing." But to the contrary, with Articles 10 and 11 unmodified, the CWC is far worse than nothing. Instead of halting the spread of poison gas, the CWC will be aiding in its proliferation by helping countries such as Iran modernize their chemical arsenals, giving them access to our secrets for defending against poison gas attack, and giving a U.S. imprimatur to third-country transfers of dangerous chemicals and defensive technology to rogue states.

Anyone who wants a road map for how this will work needs only to examine how Russia has taken advantage of similar provisions in the Nuclear Nonproliferation Treaty. Russia is at this moment using the treaty to justify its sale of nuclear reactors to Iran under a provision known as "Atoms for Peace." Under the CWC's Articles 10 and 11—"Poisons for Peace"—if Russia or China decides, for example, to build a chemical manufacturing facility in Iran (giving that terrorist regime the chemical agents and high technology it needs to build chemical weapons), Russia and China could argue not only that they are allowed to give Iran this technology but also that they are obligated to do so under a treaty ratified by the U.S. Senate.

Worse, the Chemical Weapons Convention also requires that we share our latest advanced chemical defensive gear with these countries. Surely it is obvious to the administration why this is a bad idea. Through reverse engineering, Iran can easily figure out how to penetrate our defensive technologies. This would not only endanger our troops, increasing their risk of exposure to poison gas, it would also increase the chances of a chemical attack by undermining the deterrent value of our defenses.

Even if the Senate were able to stop such direct U.S. transfers, in contravention of our legally binding treaty obligation, this would in no way prevent other countries from sharing our technology with terrorist states. It's not hard to imagine a scenario in which a third country (France, Germany, or Russia, to name a few) that does not agree with our policy of isolating Iran, would get access to U.S. chemicals and defensive technology under the CWC and then share them with another signatory such as Iran or China, all the while remaining in full compliance with the treaty.

Worse still, once the free flow of U.S. chemical and defensive secrets between signatory nations begins, it will be impossible to prevent the transfer of these secrets to rogue states that do not sign the treaty. Can anyone really believe, for example, that Iran will not share this information with its terrorist allies Syria and Libya? As former defense secretary Donald Rumsfeld has said, "With the dramatically increased flow of information which Articles 10 and 11 require, there is no question that the information will get out into the marketplace. If that many countries have it, it will not be kept from the rogue nations." Thus, giving a signatory like Iran access to U.S. chemical technology is tantamount to sharing it directly with rogue states that refuse to sign.

Why would the United States permit such dangerous technology transfers to hostile regimes? In theory, Iran, China, and others will promise to end their chemical weapons programs in exchange. But as James Schlesinger, a former director of the CIA and secretary of defense, warned the Senate Foreign Relations Committee, anyone who believes that "must be suffering from hallucinations."

If we cannot trust them to comply, can U.S. intelligence at least verify whether they are complying with the treaty? Of course not. Even the Clinton administration admits that the treaty cannot be verified.

So if we can neither trust nor verify that these nations are giving up their chemical arms programs, why would we agree to share advanced U.S. chemicals, know-how, and defensive gear with them? That is precisely the question before the Senate this week.

The Chemical Weapons Convention is, if nothing else, a well-intentioned treaty. It will not stop the spread of chemical weapons. Still, if it did no harm, one might make a credible case for its ratification. But it does threaten harm—potentially enormous harm.

Ratifying the CWC would send a signal to the world that something has been done about the proliferation of chemical weapons when in fact we have actually made the problem much worse, because Articles 10 and 11 of this dangerously flawed treaty ensure that the CWC will increase the spread of chemical weapons rather than stopping it.

So the administration has a choice: It can accept the protections that Senator Lott and I have inserted requiring them to modify Articles 10 and 11, or it can stonewall and risk losing the CWC.

THE FLAWS IN THE CHEMICAL WEAPONS TREATY
USA Today, September 12, 1996

IF THE U.S. SENATE WERE ASKED TO VOTE to require that the United States assist Cuba and Iran in modernizing their chemical weapons facilities, most senators would be instantly opposed. Yet this is precisely what the Clinton administration is demanding that the Senate do today, when the Chemical Weapons Convention becomes the pending business. And that's just the tip of the iceberg of what is wrong with this dangerously flawed treaty.

Banning chemical weapons sounds good in theory, but the treaty will do nothing to protect the American people from the perils of poison gas. What it will do is improve rogue nations' access to chemical agents, while imposing massive new regulations on thousands of U.S. businesses, compromising their trade secrets, and exposing them to unprecedented and unconstitutional inspections by international regulators. This treaty must be rejected.

Consider: Article 11 of the treaty bars the United States or any other signatory from denying access to its chemical exports, and information or equipment involved in their production, for any nation that signs and ratifies the treaty. Nations that could demand such access include terrorist regimes in Iran and Cuba as well as known proliferators such as Russia and China.

Further, most of the nations likely to use chemical weapons in an aggressive manner are not bound by the treaty. North Korea, Libya, Iraq, and Syria—all principal sponsors of terrorism and repositories of chemical weapons—are not signatories and won't be affected. Who will be affected? American businesses—as many as eight thousand of them, according to Clinton administration estimates. And not just chemical manufacturers. Any company that produces or uses most chemicals will be liable. Industries hit by the treaty's massive new regulations include the automotive, paint and varnish, electronics, textiles, food processor, soap and detergent, and cosmetics industries. This treaty will hurt Mary Kay far more than Saddam Hussein.

Under this flawed treaty, inspectors from an international regulatory agency based in The Hague can descend on any or all of these companies, without probable cause, without a search warrant, and practically without notice. They can interrogate employees and demand access to their records, equipment, and chemicals. They will be authorized to remove documents and chemical samples from the premises. Not only is this unconstitutional, it also is an invitation to industrial espionage.

Worse still, the treaty is unverifiable, as the intelligence community has already made clear. Why? Because most prohibited activity can be easily concealed or disguised.

Consider: When verifying compliance with nuclear weapons treaties, the intelligence community does not follow nuclear material; it watches the means of delivery—missiles, silos, bomber configurations. But how does one follow the means of delivery when it is a lunch pail filled with Sarin left on a Tokyo subway car? How does one track weapons produced in an eight-by-ten room in downtown Baghdad, Tehran, Pyongyang, or even Tokyo?

Further, the direct costs to the taxpayers will be astronomical. The United States must pay 25 percent of the costs of implementation and verification of the treaty—potentially billions of dollars. In addition, U.S. taxpayers will be required to provide massive new foreign aid outlays to assist Moscow in its chemical-destruction program. Prime Minister Chernomyrdin wrote Vice President Gore last month informing him that Russia would participate in the treaty only if the United States agrees to pay Russia's compliance costs. The Russian embassy estimates these to be roughly $5.5 billion. In reality, it will be as much as double or triple this amount because Russia has vastly underreported the size of its chemical stockpiles.

Some proponents have argued that, even if it won't work, even with these enormous costs to businesses and taxpayers, ratifying the treaty sends a "moral signal." The treaty, they say, is better than nothing. They are wrong. It is, in fact, far worse than nothing because ratifying the treaty will lull the world into a false sense of security that we have actually done something to deal with the proliferation of chemical weapons.

That is why many respected constitutional and foreign policy leaders have come forward in opposition to the treaty, including Dick Cheney, Jeane Kirkpatrick, Caspar Weinberger, William Clark, Robert Bork, and Edwin Meese III. They oppose this treaty because they see what we all should see: that the treaty will not accomplish its stated goals. It will increase access to chemical weapons by rogue states, it will cost taxpayers billions in new foreign aid, and in the process it will devastate American businesses with new regulations, inspections, and loss of trade secrets.

That is far too high a price to pay so that Bill Clinton can falsely claim to have saved the world from the scourge of chemical weapons.

Part II
...*And Her Moral Mission*

Chapter 6
A Moral Foreign Policy

AMERICA MUST STAND FOR MORE THAN JUST PROFIT—it must stand for American values. In this essay, written for *Foreign Affairs* magazine, Senator Helms expresses his deep dismay at the crusade by some in the business community to get rid of economic sanctions on nations that abuse human rights and proliferate weapons of mass destruction.

Sanctions, along with war and diplomacy, are the main tools of American foreign policy. He chastises those in the business community who would remove this vital tool from America's foreign policy arsenal and lead our country into an amoral, mercantilist foreign policy.

—————

WHAT SANCTIONS EPIDEMIC?
Foreign Affairs, **January–February 1999**

IN THE PAST YEAR A HANDFUL of Washington business lobbyists have waged a blistering campaign to persuade the world that Congress has been engaged in a spasm of sanctions proliferation.

Reliance on unilateral sanctions, these lobbyists warn us, is a disturbing new epidemic. Their campaign has sparked dozens of news articles and editorials decrying the "sanctions frenzy" and castigating Congress's "voracious appetite" for sanctions. Normally responsible journalists parrot statistics—conveniently furnished by these business lobbyists—alleging that in the past few years the United States has placed anywhere from one-half to two-thirds of the world's population under the yoke of unilateral economic sanctions. The *New York Times* clamors that "more than 60 laws or executive orders authorizing sanctions...have been enacted in the last five years." Even President Clinton jumped on the antisanctions bandwagon, announcing in 1998 that the United States has gone "sanctions happy."

This is sheer nonsense. The statistics peddled by these lobbyists are grossly inflated and intentionally misleading. Half of the world is not living under American sanctions—nowhere near it. There is no epidemic. Congress has been cautious and circumspect, passing just a handful of carefully targeted sanctions laws. And unilateral economic sanctions are by no means new: They have been vital weapons in America's foreign policy arsenal for more than two hundred years. I have been and continue to be a friend of American business. But the distortions spread by this small cabal of lobbyists in the name of American business are inexcusable. The time has come for a reality check.

The statistic has become conventional wisdom: In just four years the United States has imposed sanctions sixty-one times, burdening 2.3 billion people (42 percent of the world). That would be pretty awful, save for one thing—it is not true. These figures have been circulated by the antisanctions business group USA Engage, based on a study by the National Association of Manufacturers (NAM). They are a fabrication. At my request, the Congressional Research Service (CRS) evaluated the NAM claim that from 1993 through 1996, "61 U.S. laws and executive actions were enacted authorizing unilateral sanctions for foreign policy purposes." CRS reported that it "could not defensibly" justify the number. "We find the calculation used in...the NAM study to be flawed, even if the specific [sanctions] were fairly characterized, which is not always the case," CRS concluded.

How did NAM come up with sixty-one sanctions? The study alleges that twenty laws were passed by Congress and forty-one were imposed by presidential action. This is a gross distortion. Nearly three-quarters of the congressional measures were not sanctions at all but conditions, limitations, or restrictions on U.S. foreign aid. One measure placed conditions on assistance to the Palestine Liberation Organization. Another barred aid for military or police training to Haitians involved in drug trafficking or human rights abuses. One "sanction" blocked assistance to countries knowingly harboring fugitives wanted by the international war crimes tribunals for Rwanda and the former Yugoslavia. Still another prohibited Defense Department aid to countries supporting terrorists. Are these the measures that NAM and USA Engage want Congress to curtail? Let's hope not.

But what about those forty-one "sanctions" imposed by the executive branch? Five are not unilateral, as NAM charges, but rather represent U.S. compliance with UN Security Council sanctions—multilateral, by definition. In seven cases, the NAM study counts the same sanction repeatedly, identifying it each time as a separate sanction. For example, the measure declaring Sudan a terrorist state is counted five different times. NAM lists two cases when no sanction was ever imposed, including a November 1994 executive order that even NAM concedes in fine print "did not impose any specific new sanctions on any countries." Eight cases represent mere restrictions on U.S. foreign aid. Five are limited bans affecting only military exports to Zaire, Nigeria, Sudan, Haiti, and Angola. Thirteen affect only a specific foreign company or person—not an entire country, not an entire industry, but one specific entity: for example, banning imports from the Chinese Qinghai Hide and Garment Factory for its use of prison slave labor or seizing the assets of individual Colombian drug traffickers.

These actions are obviously not what most people think of as "sanctions." They think instead of broad trade bans affecting whole countries, entire industries, vast populations, or access to large markets—not conditioning U.S. foreign aid, blocking imports from a single prison factory in China, seizing the assets of drug barons, or halting the sale of lethal weapons to terrorist states.

The claim that 42 percent of the world's population has been affected is also bogus. The study lists the entire population of the former Zaire (now the Congo) as being under U.S. sanction because the United States barred sales of defense items to the government. The same goes for China, Nigeria, Mauritania, and Pakistan, where CRS notes that such highly targeted actions "put the entire populations of these countries into NAM's calculation, even though most people...are not likely to experience significant impact from or awareness of [the] imposition." American access to those countries' commercial goods-and-services markets remains unaffected.

What is the reality? Between 1993 and 1996, Congress passed and the president signed a grand total of five new sanctions laws: the Nuclear Proliferation Prevention Act of 1994, the Cuban Liberty and Democratic Solidarity Act of 1996, the Antiterrorism and Effective Death Penalty Act of 1996, the Iran-Libya Sanctions Act of 1996, and the Free Burma Act of 1996. During the same period, the president imposed just four new sanctions: declaring Sudan a terrorist state; banning imports of munitions and ammunition from China; tightening travel-related restrictions, cash remittance levels, and the sending of gift parcels to Cuba (restrictions that have since been lifted); and imposing a ban on new contractual agreements or investment in Iran. Nine new sanctions. That is it. The allegation of a sanctions epidemic is demonstrably false—a myth spread with the intention of misleading Congress, the American public, and the American business community.

Even more telling is what the business lobbyists leave out of their inflated inventory of sanctions. As they rail against "unilateral economic sanctions for foreign policy purposes" (NAM's phrase), they conveniently omit discussing unilateral economic sanctions for trade purposes. Retaliatory trade sanctions are not mentioned by NAM and are not covered by the proposed Sanctions Reform Act—a stunning admission of the efficacy of sanctions. After all, if unilateral sanctions did not work, why on earth would business want to protect the U.S. ability to impose them in trade disputes? The ability to threaten and impose unilateral economic sanctions is a vital tool of U.S. trade policy, just as it is in U.S. foreign policy.

What these lobbyists really dislike is not the idea of sanctions themselves but the reason some sanctions are imposed. They tacitly admit that sanctions work but insist that sanctions are good only if they defend business interests, not national interests. According to the lobbyists, the United States should be hamstrung when a government proliferates weapons of mass destruction, commits genocide, tortures its people, or supports terrorists. But if that same government floods the American market with cheap television sets, America should throw the book at it. But, of course, the business lobbyists cannot say that, so they attempt to confuse the issue with cooked-up data claims of an epidemic. They establish groups with clever monikers like "USA Engage," whose very name implies that those who disagree with them are isolationists. But what they really stand for is not engagement but mercantilism—an amoral foreign policy.

Sanctions have always been an American foreign policy weapon. The American colonies imposed economic sanctions against Britain in response to the Stamp and Townshend Acts, in both cases forcing their repeal. Jefferson and Madison both passionately advocated economic sanctions, believing not only that they were legitimate but also that they should be America's primary diplomatic tools. In an 1805 letter to Jefferson, Madison argued, "The efficacy of an embargo...cannot be denied. Indeed, if a commercial weapon can be properly crafted for the Executive hand, it is more and more apparent to me that it can force nations...to respect our rights." Jefferson, for his part, contended that in foreign affairs "three alternatives alone are to be chosen from: 1. Embargo. 2. War. 3. Submission and tribute."

Jefferson was right. There are indeed three tools in foreign policy: diplomacy, sanctions, and war. Take away sanctions and how can the United States deal with terrorists, proliferators, and genocidal dictators? Our options would be empty talk or sending in the marines. Without sanctions the United States would be virtually powerless to influence events absent war. Sanctions may not be perfect and they are not always the answer, but they are often the only weapon.

Unilateral sanctions, in fact, are the linchpin of our nonproliferation policy. According to a recently declassified analysis by the Arms Control and Disarmament Agency, "The history of U.S.-China relations shows that China has made specific nonproliferation commitments only under the threat or imposition of sanctions." Short of war, sanctions are the main leverage the United States has over China.

They have also played a crucial role in trade disputes. The threat of unilateral sanctions on China over intellectual property rights and unfair trade barriers has forced China several times to yield. In November 1991 the U.S. trade representative threatened $1.5 billion in trade sanctions if an intellectual property rights agreement was not reached by January 1992. Not surprisingly, such an agreement was struck on January 16, 1992. No wonder business lobbyists are so keen to retain unilateral sanctions in the trade arsenal—even as they campaign to remove them from our nation's foreign policy.

U.S. sanctions helped bring down the Soviet Union. They played a pivotal role in forcing communist Poland to release political prisoners and legalize Solidarity—sparking the collapse of communism. Our targeted Nigerian sanctions are beginning to bear fruit as the military government wearies of its pariah status. In Guatemala, the decision to freeze $47 million in U.S. aid (one of the "sanctions" that business is lobbying to curtail) and the mere threat of lost trade convinced business, labor, and military leaders to roll back President Jorge Serrano Elias's May 1993 coup. Swiss banks' recent decision to pay $1.25 billion in reparations to Holocaust survivors was a direct result of threatened sanctions, as admitted by the Union Bank of Switzerland.

Critics respond that sanctions have failed to bring down regimes in Iraq, Iran, Syria, Sudan, Libya, and Cuba. Perhaps—but they have effectively contained the Saddam Husseins, Mu'ammar al-Qadhafis, and Hafez al-Assads of the world. Without sanctions, Saddam would now be threatening the world with VX missiles, Qadhafi would be blowing up U.S. passenger planes, and Assad would be planning terrorist operations against U.S. citizens. If this policy represents failure, it beats capitulation any day. As for Cuba, until 1991 the U.S. embargo was offset by $5 billion to $7 billion in Soviet subsidies. Only without them has the embargo begun to take a toll on Castro's regime. The moment the embargo kicked in, Castro's efforts to finance Marxist insurgencies stopped, allowing the nearly complete democratic transformation of the Western Hemisphere. Castro's regime is teetering; unless America gives up its leverage by unconditionally lifting the embargo, his successors will be anxious to exchange normalized relations with the United States for a democratic transition in Cuba.

When sanctions do not work, it is often because the target government doubts our resolve to keep them imposed. And with good reason: The Clinton administration views sanctions as domestic public relations tools rather than as foreign policy weapons. For example, President Clinton signed the Iran-Libya Sanctions Act live on CNN. But once the camera lights dimmed and the time came to implement it, he lost his nerve. This sent the message to Iran and other rogue states that the administration talks tough but caves in under pressure. It is the same with Cuba. After the Castro regime murdered four innocent people, including three Americans, by shooting down two civilian planes flying over international waters, Clinton made a bold speech for the cameras and signed the Helms-Burton law. Since then, he has done everything in his power to avoid enforcing it. Clinton has also gone to extraordinary lengths to avoid imposing sanctions on China for its missile proliferation, despite incontrovertible evidence from American intelligence that sanctionable activities have taken place.

Congress has given the president great flexibility in most U.S. sanctions laws. National interest waivers let the White House temporarily or permanently suspend prescribed sanctions. Even so, when the administration feels Congress has set the bar too high for these waivers, it can get around it by, as President Clinton recently said, "fudg[ing] an evaluation of the facts." If anything, Congress has already given the president too much flexibility.

Ironically, those who criticize sanctions as a one-size-fits-all foreign policy propose a worse solution—the Sanctions Reform Act. This cookie-cutter legislation is no solution at all. Instead of providing greater flexibility on sanctions policy—the clarion call of the reform crowd—this law does the exact opposite by tying the hands of both Congress and the president.

The bill prohibits the president from implementing any sanctions for a mandatory forty-five-day "cooling-off" period. That may sound reasonable, but in practice, placing a six-week shackle on all U.S. sanctions in every situation and circumstance is dangerous folly. Ponder one example: After Libyan terrorists blew up Pan Am flight 103, the United Nations spent months debating appropriate sanctions. Meanwhile, Libya divested itself of all its reachable assets, thereby avoiding the sanctions' impact. The Sanctions Reform Act would essentially afford other terrorist states the same courtesy. While the United States "cools off" for six weeks, terrorists, proliferators, and dictators will take evasive measures—quietly divesting assets, concealing evidence, and finding safe haven for fugitives.

The Sanctions Reform Act would also impose a mandatory two-year "sunset" on all new U.S. sanctions. Another bad idea. A two-year sunset writes "sanctions fatigue" into law, sending the target state a clear message: Hunker down and wait out the storm, since U.S. resolve will collapse on a fixed date. The bill also mandates the sanctity of contracts. Again, this sounds reasonable, but it is not. What happens if a U.S. company contracts to sell militarily sensitive technology to a country that suddenly tests a nuclear bomb (India, Pakistan), invades a neighbor (Iraq), engages in genocide (Serbia), or commits an act of terrorism (Iran, Libya)? The Sanctions Reform Act would prevent the United States from breaching the contract by stopping those militarily sensitive sales.

None of this means that the United States should never protect existing business contracts with sanctioned states. In most cases, it does just that. The Clinton administration's recent executive order imposing new sanctions on Iran bars only "new investments and contracts." The Helms-Burton law affects only those investments made in stolen U.S. properties in Cuba after the date of its enactment. But Congress and the White House should decide these matters case by case and not be tied down by a mandatory provision that could have unintended consequences.

Congress already has a system for considering U.S. economic sanctions. It is called congressional debate. Each sanctions law is considered carefully, every provision is debated openly, and varying levels of flexibility are written into the law. Business gets a chance to weigh in, as do other constituencies. In the end, the president can veto any law. And Congress can always go back and amend sanctions if necessary—as it just did with India and Pakistan. The system the Founders established to decide such matters works just fine. It does not need "reform" inspired by a "sanctions epidemic" fabricated in some Washington lobbying firm's offices.

Why have some American companies invested so much in fighting sanctions? In Europe, business and government opposition to sanctions is understandable. Slumping welfare-state economies and double-digit unemployment drive Europeans to employ increasingly trade-obsessed foreign policies. But American business has no such excuse. Thanks to the vigilance of congressional Republicans, they have not been saddled with high taxes and regulations. The U.S. economy is booming, and unemployment is at an all-time low.

The lobbyists' cry that sanctions cost the United States vital access to large markets is a sham. The cost of U.S. sanctions is minuscule. According to Jan Paul Acton of the Congressional Budget Office (CBO), "To date, the cost of existing sanctions to the overall economy has been quite modest. CBO's review of research indicates that the net cost may be less than $1 billion annually. That compares with $6.6 trillion of total national income in 1997." The United States gave away roughly $13 billion in foreign aid during 1997. Besides, cutting foreign aid to punish misbehavior actually saves taxpayers' money. Even if we use the business lobbyists' standard tactic of applying costs to entire populations, the price tag for U.S. economic sanctions comes to a whopping $3.77 per American—about the cost of a Big Mac and fries.

That is a small price to pay for a moral foreign policy—and a price most Americans are willing to bear. A 1998 *Wall Street Journal*/NBC News poll taken on the eve of the president's visit to China showed that less than one-third of Americans agreed that "we should maintain good trade relations with China, despite disagreements we might have with its human rights policies." Fully two-thirds of Americans agreed that "we should demand that China improve its human rights policies if China wants to continue to enjoy its current trade status with the United States."

This may shock the business lobbyists. It should not. Americans do not need to sell their souls or their national security to create jobs and economic prosperity. The lobbyists behind this antisanctions crusade are saying, "If you can't beat 'em, join 'em." America cannot stop rogue states from acquiring weapons of mass destruction, they say, so why cede markets for sensitive technology to our European competitors? The United States cannot stop dictators from torturing people, so why not close our eyes and trade with them as if nothing is happening? That is not the American way. Americans do not need to create jobs by selling thumbscrews to the world's tyrants.

U.S. policies should isolate terrorist regimes like Iran, Iraq, Libya, Syria, and Cuba. U.S. aid should not go to countries that commit genocide, harbor war criminals, support terrorism, or export illegal drugs that poison American children. Lethal weapons should not be sold to violent regimes in Nigeria and Sudan; assets of drug traffickers should be seized; imports from Chinese companies that use prison slave labor should be banned; and government procurement contracts should not be given to foreign companies that sell dangerous technologies to terrorist states. There should be sanctions on companies and governments that proliferate nuclear, chemical, and biological weapons and countries that murder women and children and pile them into mass graves. America should not hesitate for one second to place a cost on these reprehensible acts to restrain those few American companies who would actually conduct business with the perpetrators of such heinous crimes.

With their antisanctions crusade, these lobbyists are fighting for business as usual with thugs, tyrants, and terrorists. They do not represent the views of the American people or most American businesses. They should be ashamed.

Chapter 7
China

DURING THE COLD WAR, the U.S. relationship with Communist China was driven by our strategic interests. The greater enemy was the Soviet Union, and the enemy of our enemy was our friend. As Ronald Reagan once put it, "I think the Red Chinese are a bunch of murdering bums...but in the big chess game going on, Russia is still the head man on the other side [and] we need a little elbow room."

Since the end of the Cold War, however, that rationale has disappeared. U.S. policy toward China is now driven almost exclusively by commercial interests. Senator Helms believes it should be driven primarily by America's moral and national security interests.

In the wake of revelations that China stole technology for every missile in the United States nuclear arsenal, Senator Helms believes the time has come for a top-to-bottom reassessment of our relations with Communist China. In these essays he discusses how that relationship should be restructured, our relationship with Taiwan, America's responsibilities in post-1997 Hong Kong, and how America's blind financing of the Communist Chinese regime will one day come back to haunt us.

TWO CHINESE STATES
Washington Post, March 31, 2000

CHEN SHUI-BIAN'S ELECTION as president of the Republic of China on Taiwan dramatically and instantly raised the stakes for U.S. policy in the Taiwan Strait.

Lee Teng-hui's election in 1996 was the first direct, popular election of a head of state in Chinese history. President-elect Chen's election marks the first peaceful transfer of power from a ruling Chinese party to its democratic opposition.

Taiwan's democratic transformation, begun by President Lee, is complete. The Republic of China's experiment in democracy is no longer an experiment—it is a proven reality. The nation that was known for the better part of forty years as "Nationalist China" now is "Democratic China."

No wonder Beijing feels so threatened.

Beijing is worried about the precedent that the people of Taiwan have set. For the past decade, mainland officials have justified their tyrannical rule by dismissing Taiwan's democracy as a ruse. The Nationalists (they told people on the mainland) have held power for forty years, just as we have held power for forty years.

No longer. Taiwan's democracy can never again be dismissed so easily, and Beijing is nervous that people on the mainland may now begin to ask, "What about us?"

That is why, in the days leading up to Taiwan's election, mainland officials sought desperately to scare Taiwanese voters into rejecting Chen. Premier Zhu Rongji went so far as to warn the people of Taiwan that if they elected Chen, they "won't get another opportunity to regret."

The people of Taiwan told Zhu what he could do with his threats. Now it is the United States' responsibility to ensure that

Zhu can never fulfill his threat to make Chen's election the final democratic election in China.

For eight years, the Clinton administration has tried to buy peace in the Taiwan Strait by kowtowing to the Chinese Communists and suggesting incredibly that Hong Kong and Macau could serve as models for Taiwan's reunification. Beijing's response has been to engage in a massive military buildup aimed at Taiwan and issue new threats against the island, dramatically lowering the bar for an armed invasion. Yet the administration sticks doggedly by its Chamberlainesque approach, promising this year to reward China's belligerent behavior by seeking permanent Most Favored Nation status for China, while doing absolutely nothing to recognize Taiwan's achievements or help Taiwan deter Chinese aggression.

Those who support economic engagement with China must recognize the Clinton policy for what it is—appeasement. Continuing it in the wake of Chen Shui-bian's election is a recipe for disaster. We must have a new approach.

Such a new U.S. approach to Taiwan must have two dimensions: a security dimension, designed to close off Beijing's avenues to destructive behavior; and a political dimension, which recognizes Taiwan's democratic development and seeks to bring Taiwan out of its international isolation.

A new policy must also recognize that the military balance of power of the past twenty years—when it was widely assumed that Taiwan had air superiority and could thereby thwart any attempted invasion or blockade by the mainland—is quickly shifting in Beijing's favor. China is adding fifty missiles a year along the coast of Taiwan in preparation for an attack and has just begun acquiring Russian destroyers armed with advanced "sunburn" missiles. According to the Pentagon, within five years China will have attained air superiority over Taiwan and will be capable of enforcing a blockade of the island.

The United States must make clear to Beijing that there is no military option in dealing with Taiwan by (1) approving Taiwan's full defense request, including AIM-120 air defense missiles, diesel submarines, and Aegis destroyers with early warning radars; (2) sharing theater missile defense technology with the aim of bringing Taiwan under a regional missile defense umbrella; (3) passing the Taiwan Security Enhancement Act, which will junk antiquated restrictions prohibiting senior U.S. officers from visiting Taiwan, expand the advice our experts can give them, and establish direct, secure communications between our two militaries.

The United States can help Chen restart the cross-strait dialogue only by allowing Taiwan to engage the mainland on the basis of "peace through strength." A renewed dialogue with Beijing can be successful only if it is undertaken on the basis of political strength as well. Just as East and West Germany were part of "one Germany," they were nonetheless separate "states." The same holds true for the two Korean states and for the two Chinese states—the People's Republic of China in Beijing and the Republic of China on Taiwan.

Accepting this objective reality does not require abandoning the possibility of reunification. Just as the two German states eventually reunited under democracy, so too do we hope that the two Chinese states may one day reunite under democracy.

Until then, the United States can no longer continue a policy pretending that the twenty-two million people of Taiwan do not exist. The United States must recognize the reality of two Chinese states by championing Taiwan's gradual entry, alongside Communist China, into international organizations, such as the World Trade Organization, the World Health Organization, and eventually the United Nations.

Chen Shui-bian's election should serve as a wake-up call to the United States and the world: "Democratic China" has arrived and demands recognition.

WHAT ARE WE GOING TO DO ABOUT CHINA?
Wall Street Journal, July 8, 1999

THANKS TO THE COX REPORT'S REVELATIONS, Americans now know that Communist China has moved almost overnight from a 1950s nuclear capability to the most modern, advanced technology in the American nuclear arsenal. It is the most devastating intelligence failure in American history.

But while the details of the report have been widely discussed, one question remains unanswered: What are we going to do about it?

China's apologists in Washington have quickly circled their wagons in an attempt to limit the impact of the Cox Report's damning disclosures on the Clinton administration's "engagement" policy toward Beijing. Incredibly, some in the administration have even had the gall to attempt to use this scandal of their own making to press for ratification of the Comprehensive Test Ban Treaty. If anyone believes that flimsy arms control agreement will restrain China's now-exposed nuclear ambitions, there's a bridge in Hong Kong I want to sell him.

The administration can no longer spin its way out of a fundamental reassessment of its China policy. The time has come for President Clinton to confront some uncomfortable facts about how China views the United States and about how the United States must respond to protect its vital interests in Asia.

China is not interested in a "strategic partnership" with the United States, as the spate of anti-American, government-sponsored riots all across China (following NATO's accidental bombing in May of the Chinese embassy in Belgrade) demonstrated. To the contrary, the Chinese regime views America as an adversary, perhaps an outright enemy. No country truly interested in a "strategic partnership" with America would mislead its people into believing that the bombing was deliberate or would refuse to broadcast American apologies—and then incite mobs to attack U.S. diplomatic posts with rocks and Molotov cocktails.

Beijing's paramount goal is to displace U.S. influence in the Asia-Pacific region. China's aim is to undermine U.S. relations with its Asian allies (who they hope will increasingly turn to China as the region's security guarantor) and prevent America from defending its vital interests in Asia—particularly our ability, and willingness, to defend Taiwan against forced reunification with the mainland.

China is determined to modernize its military forces, especially its nuclear capabilities, speedily in order to challenge U.S. military dominance in the Pacific. The Chinese know that today their military is vastly inferior to ours, but as their military might increases, we can be sure that the Chinese regime will act more assertively.

China's nuclear espionage has brought us significantly closer to the day when Beijing will be in a position to use nuclear blackmail against the United States. China has already shown its willingness to issue such threats. Just after China fired missiles off Taiwan's coast in 1995, a Chinese general publicly boasted that the United States would never come to Taiwan's defense because Americans "care more about Los Angeles than Taipei."

Of course, China does not want open war with America. As the Chinese philosopher Sun Tzu wrote some 2,500 years ago in *The Art of War*, "Supreme excellence in war consists in breaking the enemy's resistance without fighting." With what Sun Tzu called a "sheathed sword"—in this case, a nuclear sword—China hopes to develop the military capacity to prevent America from defending its interests in Asia.

Those who argue for U.S. "engagement" with China delude themselves if they daydream that America can engage China from a position of weakness. Ronald Reagan's dictum of peace through strength applies as much in the Far East as it did in the East Bloc. We can convince the Chinese leadership to behave only if its avenues to adventurism and confrontation are closed. To start, we must take the following steps:

First, shore up our own defenses, and those of our allies, in the region. The most urgent priority is Taiwan. With Hong Kong back in the fold and Macau soon to be reabsorbed into the mainland, Beijing's leaders now view the reunification of Taiwan as their number one priority. That is why the U.S. Senate must approve the bipartisan Taiwan Security Enhancement Act. The act will authorize more U.S. arms sales to Taiwan and increase cooperation between the U.S. and Taiwanese militaries. This will deter Chinese threats against the island. And given China's recent seizures of islands that lie within Philippine maritime boundaries, it is also imperative that we rebuild our defense relationship with the Philippines, now that the Philippine Senate has ratified the Visiting Forces Agreement.

Second, we must bring Taiwan under a regional missile defense umbrella that will protect the Taiwanese, and all U.S. allies in the region, from ballistic missile attack by China (or for that matter by North Korea). This is vital because during the past year China has begun moving hundreds of medium-range ballistic missiles along the coast near the Taiwan Strait, in a clear effort to intimidate Taipei.

Third and foremost, the United States must move quickly to build a national missile defense to protect the American people from ballistic missile attack. China can't blackmail us with nuclear weapons if its missiles can't hit the United States. We must, once and for all, place that antiquated Cold War relic known as the Anti-Ballistic Missile Treaty into the dustbin of history and then build and deploy a system to defend us from the threat of Chinese ballistic missile attack.

Thanks to this administration's ineptitude, China now possesses the most advanced American nuclear weapons technology. The leaders in Beijing must be made to know, in no uncertain terms, that they will never be able to use that technology to intimidate the United States. Then, and only then, can we have any sort of con-structive "engagement" with them.

RED CHINA, FREE CHINA
Apple Daily (Hong Kong), November 15, 1999

TAIWAN'S DEMOCRATICALLY ELECTED PRESIDENT, Lee Teng-hui, merely stated the obvious when he declared earlier this year that China is a divided nation made up of two separate and sovereign "states." His statements regarding Taiwan's status—recently spelled out in the journal *Foreign Affairs*—are undeniably true, obvious to all except Red China's dictators (and a handful of American "China experts"), who wish to preserve the fiction that Taiwan is a "renegade province" of the People's Republic of China.

Just as both East and West Germany were part of "Germany," they were nonetheless separate states. The same is true of the People's Republic of China in Beijing and the Republic of China on Taiwan. And, just as the two German states eventually reunited under democracy, so too do we hope that the two Chinese states can one day reunite—under democracy.

But instead of supporting President Lee, the Clinton administration chose instead to parrot Beijing's fictional diplomatic constructions about Taiwan's status. Worse, President Clinton even suggested that Hong Kong's reunification with Red China under the "one country, two systems" construction could be a model for Taiwan's eventual reunification with the mainland.

Of course, the U.S. Congress will never allow such an abandonment of America's friends on Taiwan. And the United States has since made clear to Beijing that any use of force against Taiwan would necessitate an American military response.

But the very fact that President Clinton would even venture such a delirious suggestion discloses his fundamental misreading of history.

As the rest of the world moves toward democracy, Beijing's aging dictators struggle daily to maintain power by suppressing internal dissent. This may buy them some time, but in the long run it cannot possibly save their crumbling system. How stable can the PRC really be if it is threatened by a peaceful spiritual movement such as Falun Gong?

The fact is, Chinese communism, like Soviet communism before it, is doomed to the ash heap of history. Red China is a dinosaur, with nothing new to offer the Chinese people. Beijing's tyrants represent China's past; Taipei's free-market democracy represents China's future.

For years we in America have been told by Red China's apologists that our insistence on democracy and human rights in China is a form of cultural imperialism. "Asian values," we are told, are different from "Western values." Chinese people, we are lectured, don't care about democracy and freedom—they place order above freedom.

Well, the Republic of China on Taiwan has laid waste to that "Asian values" nonsense on which the Chinese communists have tried to justify their totalitarian rule.

Twenty years ago, Taiwan was under martial law. Today, it is a vibrant, multiparty democracy, with a spirited opposition, a free press, and a flourishing civil society. The Chinese people on Taiwan have shown the world that their democracy—and not Red China's communist tyranny—is the model for the future of Chinese civilization.

On the economic front, Taiwan is flourishing while Beijing is floundering. The Republic of China's free-market policies have helped make Taiwan not only one of the freest but also one of the richest nations in the world.

Unlike its communist neighbor, which has sought to contain the virus of capitalism inside Special Economic Zones (with internal borders that isolate the vast majority of Chinese citizens from the effects of the free market), Taiwan has warmly embraced both economic and political freedom for all of Taiwan's people. As a result, the Republic of China has become the model of success for Chinese people everywhere.

Of course, it is the Chinese people on Taiwan who deserve the credit for this fantastic political and economic achievement. But it is fair to say that U.S. support, through the Taiwan Relations Act, has played a critical role. Through the Taiwan Relations Act, the United States officially recognized the democratic aspirations of the people on Taiwan. The act helped maintain a stable economic and trade climate between our two countries. It let the people of Taiwan know that, despite so-called "de-recognition," the United States was not going to allow them to be treated as a renegade appendage of Communist China. And the defense provisions of the Taiwan

Relations Act put Red China on notice that the United States expects it to keep its hands off our friends.

Now, as we prepare to enter a new century in which Beijing's threats to Taiwan are certain to grow, it is vital that the United States take steps to further support our democratic friends in Taiwan and make clear to Beijing that forced reunification is not an option.

With Hong Kong and Macau both under Red China's sovereignty at the close of 1999, reunification of Taiwan will soon become Beijing's top agenda item. And today, sensing the Clinton administration's boundless desire to appease them, the Chinese communists are ramping up the pressure as never before for America to abandon Taiwan.

The Clinton administration has been happy to play along. Just last summer, President Clinton caved in to Beijing's "three noes" demand (no Taiwan recognition, no Taiwan independence, no Taiwan membership in international organizations). And I must confess, I am fearful that our arms sales to Taiwan will be sacrificed next—unless we do something to stop it.

This is why I have introduced the Taiwan Security Enhancement Act. This bipartisan legislation seeks to ensure that our friends in the Republic of China will have the equipment to maintain their self-defense capabilities, by prohibiting any and all politically motivated reductions in arms sales to Taiwan pursuant to the 1982 Communiqué and by authorizing the sale of a broad array of defense weaponry to Taiwan.

The Taiwan Security Enhancement Act also proposes to redress some of the deficiencies in the Republic of China's military readiness that stem in part from the twenty-year isolation of Taiwan's military. For instance, when Red Chinese missiles were flying over Taiwan in 1996 and our carriers went to the strait, Taiwan's military had no direct, secure way of communicating with our fleet. That's because Taiwan's military does not conduct military exercises with us or engage in planning with us. Indeed, the State Department prevents any U.S. officer above the rank of colonel from setting foot on Taiwan. Not only is this outrageous, but it also undermines America's ability to deter conflict in the Taiwan Strait.

The Taiwan Relations Act calls for the United States—not Taiwan, but the United States—to maintain a capacity to resist any resort to force or coercion that would jeopardize Taiwan. But this is difficult if we don't train, plan, or communicate with Taiwan's military.

The Taiwan Security Enhancement Act will change this by increasing participation by Taiwan at our defense colleges, requiring the enhancement of our military exchanges, and establishing direct communications between our two militaries.

Now, some people, as can always be expected, call this bill provocative. They have said that doing these things will upset Communist China. Of course they will. But if anyone needs evidence of the need for such legislation, Red China's recent behavior is a clear warning in that regard.

The massive and threatening military buildup by Communist China—much of it aimed at Taiwan—should make clear to all that this is certainly no time to reduce our arms sales to Taiwan. To the contrary, it is exactly time to review our defense relationship with Taiwan and to find ways in which that relationship can be enhanced so as to deter any provocative actions on the part of Beijing.

For two decades, the Taiwan Relations Act has made clear to the dictators in Beijing, and to the people on Taiwan, that America's friendship with, and commitment to, the Republic of China remains strong.

Now, as we prepare to enter a new century in which Communist China is sure to increase its pressure on Taiwan dramatically, it is incumbent upon us to show, in concrete ways, that our commitment to the Republic of China's security remains unchanged.

We must take steps to increase our military cooperation with Taipei and provide the Taiwanese the means of self-defense. And we must make clear to Beijing, in no uncertain terms, that peace in the Taiwan Strait and the preservation of Taiwan's democratic, free-market system are in the vital national security interests of the United States.

HONG KONG: EXIT BRITAIN, ENTER AMERICA
Asian Wall Street Journal, June 25, 1997

AT THE CEREMONIES MARKING the return of Hong Kong to China, the most important participant will not be Chinese president Jiang Zemin or British prime minister Tony Blair, but the U.S. secretary of state, Madeleine Albright. Secretary Albright's decision to go to Hong Kong, but not to attend the swearing-in of the provisional legislature on July 1, launches a new period in which the United States will no longer have the excuse of a close friendship with Britain to let China's broken promises on Hong Kong go unanswered.

In that sense, while the ceremonies will formally transfer sovereignty of Hong Kong to China, they will also signal the handover of responsibility for Hong Kong's fate to the United States.

It is mystifying indeed that the United States did not seek to influence Sino-British negotiations in the 1980s over the Joint Declaration, the handover agreement. According to Gerald Segal, author of *The Fate of Hong Kong*, "[T]he American attitude to the Hong Kong negotiations was one of an 'interested bystander.' Far from taking an active part in the fate of Hong Kong, the United States left it to Britain to hand back the colony."

Despite its growing economic stake in Hong Kong, including a large expatriate business community and export market, the United States is virtually absent from accounts of the negotiations. This was undeniably a mistake on America's part. We will never know how Hong Kong's current situation might have been different had the United States put its leverage—economic and political—behind Britain as it settled Hong Kong's future.

Nevertheless, the signing of the 1984 Joint Declaration, which established the terms under which Hong Kong would return to Chinese sovereignty, did raise America's profile in Hong Kong's affairs. The Reagan administration responded positively to the Joint Declaration itself and in other ways—for instance, by announcing that it would recognize the passports to be held by Hong Kong's citizens.

In 1992 my congressional colleagues and I passed, and President George Bush signed, the U.S.–Hong Kong Policy Act, making U.S. support for the Joint Declaration a matter of law while pledging continued close bilateral relations based on Hong Kong's autonomy from China. More significantly, the act directly linked Hong Kong's autonomy to future U.S.–Hong Kong relations by authorizing the president to determine whether Hong Kong is autonomous and, if it is not, to suspend laws according Hong Kong separate treatment from China. Therefore, if China wishes to benefit from U.S. investment, the vast majority of which goes through Hong Kong, then Beijing had better not fool around with Hong Kong's autonomy.

Congress also strongly supported Hong Kong's elections in 1991 and 1995 and criticized Chinese violations of the Joint Declaration—especially the creation of the provisional legislature, which is to replace the elected Legislative Council with the June 30 handover. Congress also focused attention on maintaining a strong bilateral relationship with Hong Kong after July 1, especially in matters of law enforcement cooperation and trade relations, areas reserved for the territory by the Sino-British agreements. Significantly, in 1989, Congress responded to the Tiananmen Square massacre, forcing the Bush administration to implement tough sanctions and to take care of students from China in the United States.

Even so, the United States has not yet gone as far as it must with regard to Hong Kong. Clearly, successive American administrations have deferred throughout the transition to Britain regarding Chinese violations of the Joint Declaration. Using the excuse that the United States "does not offer legal interpretations of agreements to which it is not a party," the stock phrase of State Department officials, the United States has watched China announce, then carry out, one violation of the Joint Declaration after another.

The United States may have refused to recognize China's broken promises out of fear that doing so would put Britain in the difficult position of turning its six million people over to the largest communist dictatorship in history according to an international agreement the United States considered breached. Britain's own violations of the Joint Declaration's guarantees for an elected legislature and an independent judiciary with the power of final adjudication presented another serious obstacle. Or possibly, U.S. deference to Britain was part of a diplomatic ploy designed to protect Washington from ever having to confront Beijing over Hong Kong.

In any event, America's loyalty to Britain over Hong Kong—though not the cost of this loyalty to Hong Kong's people—will soon be moot. In five days, Britain will be gone from Hong Kong, saying that it will take up Chinese violations of the Joint Declaration in the International Court of Justice, provided the Chinese agree.

Don't hold your breath. But whether Britain is able to pursue its agenda at international court or not, the United States will be free—and must be willing—to employ tactics well beyond legal challenges, including, for example, canceling plans to grant President Jiang a summit meeting in Washington, while imposing other kinds of political and economic pressures, until China lives up to its commitments.

I believe China recognized far earlier than the United States did that it would be up to the United States, not Britain, to secure Hong Kong's future. In *The End of Hong Kong*, Robert Cottrell recounts a shrewd forecast made by Singapore's senior minister, Lee Kuan Yew, in December 1992. Mr. Lee saw that Hong Kong governor Christopher Patten's minor expansion of representative government in the colony "might prove a stalking horse for Western pressure [on China] on other issues." At that time, China was preparing to deal with President-elect Bill Clinton, fresh from denouncing George Bush on the campaign trail for coddling the "butchers of Beijing."

Mr. Lee imagined China's likely reasoning: "If I give way on Hong Kong to the British, who do not have either the military or the economic clout to hurt me, then I am inviting trouble from Bill Clinton. Chris Patten can only express his exasperation, but Bill Clinton can turn off MFN" or apply a number of other pressures. Mr. Lee concluded: "I think it is highly unlikely, given those stakes, that [China] is going to back off."

China, of course, did not back off. Indeed, China has gone well beyond undoing Governor Patten's modest reform package, abolishing the Legislative Council outright. Through its proxies in the provisional legislature, China has unleashed a barrage of attacks on Hong Kong's civil liberties.

But Mr. Lee's supposition of an American president willing to use his leverage to protect Hong Kong and advance other U.S. interests with China has so far been off the mark. President Clinton has proved himself less, not more, willing than Mr. Bush to take a tough line with China.

Secretary Albright's decision to snub the provisional legislature shows that the administration recognizes that the fight over Hong Kong is just beginning. With Britain gone, only the United States has the will and the way to stand up for Hong Kong.

MOST FAVORED NATION?
The Weekly Standard, February 24, 1997

A REPORT PERSISTS IN WASHINGTON that the Clinton administration will soon seek permanent Most Favored Nation status for the People's Republic of China—possibly in exchange for some concessions on human rights or for shaping up on standards for admission to the World Trade Organization. The office of the U.S. trade representative has denied the report, but it is becoming more and more credible considering Clinton's references to his new "inevitability" policy, according to which the United States need not confront China over its human rights abuses or violation of agreements because China's peaceful transformation to democracy is inevitable.

Even if freedom and democracy are inevitable in China, do not expect that I will greet the first elected president of post-Communist China by saying, "I thought about depriving the old regime of economic and political benefits, but since your success was inevitable, I had Jiang Zemin and General Chi over for coffee at the Senate Foreign Relations Committee."

The inevitability theory does have one thing going for it: predictability. We can all fill in our 1997 calendars now. In mid-March, pencil in "U.S. cave-in at Geneva UN Human Rights Commission." In the last week of May, jot down "Renewal of MFN." You can be pretty specific about exactly what moment that will occur: Put it down for 6 P.M. the Friday before Memorial Day, when the administration traditionally delivers the notice just in time to make the Saturday papers but after members of Congress have left for home.

Needless to say, supporters of permanent MFN look forward to the time when the annual debate over renewal can be avoided. They decry the "sterility" of the debate. Lobbyists for business interests chortle over the "annual exercise" and smugly shake their heads at misguided anti-MFN diehards. Their attitude is that America should put a stop to the annual debate over MFN because the Chinese know we are not serious. This is a variation of the inevitability theory: "Best not to have a debate over principle among elected representatives because when the majority favoring MFN wins, it just confuses the Chinese."

The idea that it would be valuable for China to enjoy permanent MFN status rests on the myth that all trade is a moderating force on repressive regimes and encourages reform. China's MFN status was restored in 1980, yet there is no evidence that this has led to an improvement in human rights in China. The 1996 State Department human rights report, just released, acknowledges that repression in China increased last year. According to the report, human rights abuses were widespread; the government used intimidation, exile, prison terms, and other measures to silence dissent. Persecution of independent Protestant and Catholic churches intensified. Minorities, including Tibetans, who are Buddhists, and Uighurs, who are Muslims, also experienced serious repression.

China's human rights performance is dictated by the nature of the regime—an arbitrary, one-party state struggling to maintain as many aspects of totalitarianism as it can while reaping economic benefits for party leaders and the military.

In China, the government controls international trade and the economy. While the United States grants China the same trading terms we give to nations where our businessmen compete on a level playing field, China limits our access to its markets. Rushing to conclude an agreement before Madeleine Albright makes her first visit to China as secretary of state, U.S. and Chinese negotiators last week cracked open China's markets for drapes and home furnishings. Typically, negotiators declined to specify how much greater access U.S. companies will have under the agreement. The U.S.-China Business Council and other MFN proponents rarely acknowledge that the United States has a $35 to $39 billion trade deficit with China. (China says the deficit is $10 billion.)

So China is not buying American; Belgium buys more U.S. goods than China does. Who benefits from this state of affairs? The Chinese government, of course. When China does buy from the United States, it predominantly buys aircraft, power-generating equipment, computers, and telecommunications equipment. U.S. trade with China is putting sophisticated technology—including machine tools useful in making not just commercial aircraft but also bombers and missiles—in the hands of military-owned and -controlled companies. The withdrawal of MFN for China is an effective tool precisely because China needs our markets. The trade surplus figures show that China relies on our consumers to buy its products.

China's growth is raising living standards, but wealth and property do not in and of themselves enable individuals to resist arbitrary government. Law does. It restrains the government and protects the citizens. But in China, the rule of law does not exist. Entrepreneurs who run afoul of a Chinese business with official connections often find themselves not in court but in jail. American businessmen have been targets of what amounts to official extortion for attempting to enforce a contract. Even companies with an ironclad legal claim against a state-owned enterprise are left holding the bag. Revpower, an American company, has been trying since 1993 to enforce a $6 million arbitral award that China is obligated to honor as a party to international agreements.

Supporters of "engagement" claim that China will be transformed into a responsible law-abiding state by its membership in the World Trade Organization and other multilateral organizations. China's behavior disproves this theory. Receiving MFN treatment for its products has not led to a more democratic, humane, or internationally responsible China, as demonstrated by its failure to respect either its citizens or agreements on issues from intellectual property to nuclear nonproliferation to Hong Kong. Renewing MFN will continue to help China's economy and military expand and modernize, while its citizens look for crumbs.

Chapter 8
The Bosnian Freedom Fighters

IN 1995 DEBATE WAS RAGING in Washington over the war in Bosnia-Herzegovina. A UN-led peacekeeping operation had failed to protect the Bosnian people from Serb-sponsored genocide. And, through an immoral arms embargo, the United States and its allies were forcing the Bosnians to defend their nation from foreign aggression with both hands tied behind their backs.

In a series of articles in 1995 for the *Wall Street Journal*, the *Los Angeles Times*, and *USA Today*, Senator Helms made the case that U.S. policy in Bosnia was immoral. The United States needed to give up its neutrality in the face of Slobodan Milosevic's aggression, lift the embargo, and arm and train the Bosnian freedom fighters.

The day that the first article appeared, Senator Helms was walking down a hallway in the Capitol when a man he did not recognize came up to him, gave him a bear hug, thanking him for what he had written that day. It was Harris Siladjic, the prime minister of Bosnia.

Helms and then–Senate majority leader Bob Dole soon introduced legislation to provide $100 million in U.S. military assistance to the Bosnian government. The Clinton administration adamantly opposed Helms's plan. But by 1996—a year after the first of these articles appeared—the administration had announced its own "train and equip" plan for the Bosnian-Croat Federation.

Why the change of heart? The Bosnians had latched onto the Helms "arm and train" proposal and made its implementation a condition for their signing the Dayton peace agreement. Though the administration would never give

him credit, its plan was a virtual carbon copy of Helms's—and became our
only exit strategy from Bosnia.

~~~~~

APPLY THE REAGAN DOCTRINE IN BOSNIA
Wall Street Journal, June 9, 1995

BY DOWNING A U.S. F-16 FIGHTER JET and taking United Nations
forces hostage, Serb warlord Radovan Karadzic made clear what
U.S. policymakers should have recognized long ago: The Serbs have
no intention of ending their unlawful, genocidal aggression against
Bosnia. Neither moral suasion nor limited acts of force will deter
them from achieving their goal—an ethnically pure Greater Serbia.

It is time for the United States to accept reality. The UN-led,
Clinton-backed policy in Bosnia, wrong from the beginning, has
now failed. The time for neutrality has passed. We must choose
sides. The UN mission in Bosnia must withdraw, the arms embargo
on the Bosnian Muslims must be lifted—unilaterally if necessary—
and the Serbs must be driven from unlawfully conquered territory.

Critics contend that choosing sides will require sending
American troops to Bosnia. The lesson of Vietnam, they argue, is
that you can't win a war with bombing alone. They are wrong. We
can support the Bosnian government forces without getting
American ground troops embroiled in the war. To see how, look
to the successful policy that ended the national paralysis over
Vietnam, the "Reagan Doctrine."

During the 1980s, U.S. policymakers realized that confronting
the expansion of Soviet communism did not require committing
American ground troops to every flashpoint around the world. In
each country faced with Soviet aggression, there were motivated
people—freedom fighters, we called them in the 1980s—willing

to fight their own wars of liberation. They did not want us to send American soldiers; they wanted us to send financial, diplomatic, and military support so they could fight and win themselves.

In this way, the Contras in Nicaragua and the Mujahadeen in Afghanistan fought and won their own wars without the involvement of U.S. forces. It is time we began treating the Bosnian Muslims as we did the Contras and Mujahadeen—as freedom fighters engaged in a war of liberation.

The freedom fighters of Bosnia need the same things the freedom fighters in Nicaragua and Afghanistan needed:

- *Arms and resupply.* The Clinton administration should work with Congress as well as supportive countries to develop a specific package of arms and equipment for the Bosnian freedom fighters. Today, Bosnian fighters often train with wooden guns, and many have never fired a real shot before entering combat. We should provide them with an arms package that ranges from the basics—guns and ammunition—to sophisticated weaponry such as antitank weapons, artillery, night-vision equipment, and communications gear.

- *Military training.* The United States should provide military advisors to help train the Bosnians in how to use the new arms and equipment and advise them on military strategy and tactics. As we have seen in previous conflicts, such knowledge and training from the United States can mean the difference between victory and defeat.

- *Financial assistance.* In addition to subsidizing arms for the Bosnians, the United States should continue humanitarian assistance for victims of the war.

- *Intelligence sharing.* The United States should immediately begin sharing intelligence with the Bosnian government, including information on Bosnian Serb troop movements, troop strength and capabilities, military supply routes, and any support from the Milosevic regime. And the United States should provide tactical advice on how to capitalize on this information.

- *Diplomatic pressure on neighboring countries.* In Nicaragua and Afghanistan, the United States brought pressure to bear on neighboring countries—Costa Rica, Honduras, and Pakistan— to get involved. Today, the United States should exert similar pressure on Bosnia's neighbors to weigh in on the side of freedom by providing bases for training and resupply, providing listening posts for intelligence, and joining the United States in giving diplomatic support to the Bosnians.

- *Diplomatic support with European allies and the UN.* As the leader of the free world, the United States should serve as a diplomatic surrogate for the Bosnian freedom fighters, supporting their interests with the NATO allies and giving them a voice in the UN Security Council.

The reality is that we should have adopted the tools of the Reagan Doctrine from the very beginning. For the past three years, the West has forced the besieged Bosnian government to fight the Serb onslaught with both hands tied behind its back. With the complicity of the Clinton administration, the UN continues to try to force an unjust settlement on the Bosnians. The fruits of this immoral policy are the Serb takeover of more than 70 percent of Bosnia-Herzegovina and hundreds of thousands of dead and dying in a bloody, UN-created stalemate.

Last week's announcement by President Clinton that he would consider the use of U.S. ground troops for "reconfiguration and strengthening" of the UN forces—subsequently curtailed in the wake of intense congressional criticism—means that U.S. policy options now stand between maintaining the status quo and sending American soldiers to fight and die in Bosnia. Neither option is acceptable.

The United States needs, once and for all, to side decisively with the Bosnian freedom fighters. Had the United States adopted such a definite policy two or three years ago, the tools of the Reagan Doctrine would have been sufficient to turn the tide of the war. They can still do the job. There is absolutely no need to send American soldiers to do what the Bosnians themselves are willing to do—fight the ground war for the liberation of their country.

Naysayers who argue that such a policy cannot succeed in Bosnia should recall America's success in Afghanistan. If we could help the Mujahadeen drive the mighty Soviet Red Army from Kabul, surely we can help the Bosnians drive the Serbs from land the Serbs have illegally conquered. It is only a question of political will.

LET'S HELP ARM THE BOSNIANS
USA Today, July 27, 1995

THE SENATE'S VOTE TO LIFT the Bosnian arms embargo marks the beginning of the end of America's shameful policy of neutrality in the Balkan conflict. When Bosnia requests the pullout of UN forces, the embargo will be lifted and the Bosnians will at last be allowed to defend themselves.

The moment has come to develop a new policy—one that distinguishes clearly between victim and aggressor and puts the diplomatic, military, and financial resources of the United States behind the victim.

Some have argued that lifting the embargo is enough—that the United States should wash its hands of the Bosnian mess. This would be a terrible mistake. Lifting the embargo is only half the solution. The United States now must lead the Atlantic alliance in a new approach by coordinating a decisive allied response to Serbia's aggression. In the name of simple decency, our policy cannot be to "lift and run"—it must be to "lift and arm."

The time has come for the president and Congress to develop a specific package of arms for the Bosnian Muslims. The president's spokesman, Michael McCurry, recently chided senators who support arming Bosnia to "explain where the money comes from, where the arms come from, how they will get them to the Bosnian Muslims." He should know better. Congress has voted three times—1993, 1994, and 1995—to give the president a $50 million authorization for arming Bosnia. The money has gathered dust for two and a half years while Bosnia has burned and thousands of innocent men, women, and children have died.

I will make the president this offer: If he will agree to a policy of aggressively supporting Bosnia's self-defense, I will introduce an amendment to the Defense appropriations bill next week allowing him immediately to take this $50 million and use it to start an international fund to enable the Bosnian government to defend itself.

Already several Muslim countries—Turkey, Saudi Arabia, Jordan, and others—have indicated a willingness to contribute to Bosnia's defense. Along with American contributions, Bosnia can acquire the weapons and training it needs to turn back Serb aggression.

Why must the United States take such a strong stand in defense of the Bosnians? There are serious moral and strategic reasons.

First, the conflict is not a "civil war" but a war of aggression. Serbia is not merely attempting to conquer Bosnia; it is trying to "ethnically cleanse" the region of Bosnian Muslims and create a racially pure Greater Serbia. This is a policy of genocide unseen in Europe since Hitler's Final Solution. America must not stand aside and play the role of disinterested observer.

Second, over the past three years, the embargo has given radical Islamic states (such as Iran) a foothold in Europe. Responsible members of the international community, Muslim or not, have abided by the embargo. The result has been an exaggerated influence for outcast nations like Iran, unfettered by the norms of international law. More troubling still, Western indifference to Serbia's genocide of the Bosnian Muslims has bolstered Iran's otherwise laughable promotion of a Western-Muslim conflict and has helped Tehran advance its anti-Western agenda in the Muslim world. With the embargo lifted, the United States must displace Iran's influence by arming the Bosnians in concert with secular Muslim governments.

Third, the United States has a vital interest in repairing the damage done to our credibility by the Clinton administration's vacillation in Bosnia. For three years, the United States has issued threats and ultimatums to the Serbs, and for three years the Serbs have thumbed their noses at us. Western forces have been taken hostage, Bosnian civilians putatively protected by the UN have been massacred, an American pilot has been shot down, and UN "safe havens" have been overrun—all with impunity.

This ongoing series of humiliations has sent a dangerous message to the world that the United States can be defied without cost or consequence. That message has repercussions far beyond the conflict in Bosnia: It undermines every aspect of our foreign policy, from pressing North Korea to abandon its nuclear program to stopping Russia's nuclear sales to Iran—increasing the odds for dangerous confrontations. That damage must be repaired. One step in that direction will be a decisive stand against the Serbs.

The Clinton administration has recently acknowledged that, once the embargo is lifted, the United States will have a "moral responsibility" to arm and train the Bosnian government. The administration argues this will require American forces to "go into Bosnia to help equip and train the Bosnians," leading to an "Americanization" of the conflict. This is a transparent excuse for doing nothing.

There is no need to send Americans to Bosnia. During the Cold War, the United States successfully backed the Contras in Nicaragua and the Mujahadeen in Afghanistan without sending one soldier to fight on the ground. As for the notion that the United States will have to train Bosnians on Bosnian territory, the most fitting word is absurd. The Bosnians can be trained anywhere; friendly Muslim countries would undoubtedly provide bases for such training.

The president should stop making excuses. Hiding behind our allies has not worked; abdicating leadership to the UN has not worked; appeasement has not worked; and issuing empty threats has not worked. The time has come to end this isolationism in the guise of multilateralism. Pull out the UN, end the embargo, and arm and train the Bosnians. If the Clinton administration has a better idea, let's hear it. Now.

SEND ARMS, NOT TROOPS
Los Angeles Times, December 13, 1995

PRESIDENT CLINTON HAS SUGGESTED that those in Congress who oppose sending American troops to Bosnia are isolationists who "question the need for our continued active leadership in the world." He has it wrong. Congress has never questioned the need for U.S. leadership; for more than three years, Congress has pleaded for just that to resolve the Balkan crisis. The question is not whether the United States should lead but how we must lead.

I do not believe that the president's plan to commit twenty thousand American troops is the best way to lead. Sending American soldiers to serve as human trip wires in Bosnia is a bad idea and will not ensure lasting peace in the Balkans. What will guarantee an enduring peace in Bosnia is not the presence of U.S. forces but rather the presence of a credible deterrent to renewed Serbian aggression: a well-armed, well-trained Bosnian military. Regardless of whether we do send troops, our primary mission must now be to create a military balance of power by helping the Bosnian government build such a deterrent.

The president said in London this week that the United States will not participate in the arming and training of Bosnian government forces. Instead, he said, the United States will seek to enforce a complicated and, I am convinced, unworkable arms control regime in the Balkans that will seek to reduce the Serbs' weaponry while depending on others to arm the Bosnians in a limited fashion.

The president has his priorities backward. Arming and training the Bosnian Muslims is significantly more important in the long run than temporarily placing American forces between the warring parties or enforcing a random and haphazard arms control program.

American troops cannot guarantee peace in Bosnia. We pray that they will not be there a year from now, much less in five or ten years. We cannot secure the long-term viability of the Bosnian state with American soldiers. But we can help the Bosnians secure the viability of their own land with American arms, training, and military know-how.

Furthermore, we cannot depend on others to do this arming and training. First, with all due respect to the military capabilities of other interested countries, they are nowhere equal to the U.S. armed forces. Second, having Americans doing this sends an important message to anyone who might consider a future assault on the Bosnian state: that the United States recognizes the difference between victim and aggressor and is siding with the victim. This message will play an important role in bolstering the new Bosnian military deterrent. Should war resume because of renewed Serbian aggression, the Serbs must know in no uncertain terms that the United States will be firmly allied with the Bosnian government.

No one understands the importance of this better than the Bosnians. In Dayton, they sought unsuccessfully to secure a U.S. commitment to arm and train their military as a deterrent. They view American leadership in training and arming their forces as essential to an enduring peace. They are right.

Some of us have argued from the beginning that the U.S. policy should have been to lift the arms embargo, arm the Bosnian forces, and allow the Bosnians to repel Serbian aggression. By the time the Dayton talks began, the Bosnian government had clearly lost all hope that the United States and its allies would do this. Weary after fighting four years without arms or allies, the Bosnians saw no alternative to accepting the de facto partition of their nation as the price of peace.

Nobody knows whether this fragile partition will lead to anything more than a brief pause before the next round of Balkan wars. A peace that requires twenty thousand American enforcers to make it viable is, I suspect, not viable in the first place. This much is certain: The Dayton agreement will never be viable until we help the Bosnian government build its military deterrent to repel a renewed Serbian assault.

If Clinton refuses to arm the Bosnians, it will be he who abdicates American leadership in the Balkans, not Congress.

Chapter 9
Kosovo—
Getting Rid of Milosevic

THE BOSNIANS WERE NOT the only victims of Slobodan Milosevic's genocide. In 1999 Milosevic's henchmen were piling bodies into mass graves in
the Serb province of Kosovo as well.

Yet the Clinton administration was still trying to appease Milosevic, working to make him a partner for peace in the Balkans. Senator Helms opposed
this appeasement of Milosevic in Bosnia and opposed it again in his brutality
in Kosovo.

In this essay, published on the first day of the Kosovo war, Senator Helms
argues that enough is enough—the only way to achieve lasting peace in the
Balkans is to remove Milosevic from power. Here, Senator Helms offers a
bipartisan plan to do just that.

<hr>

MILOSEVIC MUST GO
Washington Post, March 25, 1999

YUGOSLAV STRONGMAN SLOBODAN MILOSEVIC has for the past
year waged a brutal campaign of genocide against the Albanian
population of Kosovo. More than six hundred thousand have been
displaced from their homes, and more than two thousand men,

women, and children have been murdered by his armed forces and interior ministry—many forced to kneel together on the ground before being sprayed with bullets and then piled into mass graves.

All this is merely the latest in Milosevic's reign of terror in the Balkans. In his proxy war against Bosnia-Herzegovina, he killed hundreds of thousands, opened the first concentration camps in Europe since the Holocaust, and almost single-handedly restored "genocide" to the European vocabulary.

American troops already have been sent into harm's way to enforce peace in Bosnia. Now, as a result of his latest repression in Kosovo, the United States is being called on again to deploy its armed forces in an even more difficult and perilous Balkan quagmire.

This must stop. And the only way it will stop—ever—is if we address the underlying cause of the problem in the Balkans: Slobodan Milosevic's continued rule. The time has come for the United States to stop coddling Milosevic and pretending that he can be part of any acceptable solution and start working toward his removal and the democratic transformation of Serbia.

Time and again the Clinton administration has sent senior envoys, such as Richard Holbrooke and Christopher Hill, to wine and dine Milosevic in the hope of convincing him to behave. Time and again he has clinked glasses and then returned to his genocidal ways.

Now, after threatening NATO air strikes twenty times without following through, the president has backed himself into a corner. So the administration is crossing its fingers and hoping air strikes will show Milosevic the error of his ways—with no idea what to do next if they don't.

Our Yugoslav policy has failed. If we are to prevent further genocide and preclude American forces from being dragged further into the Balkans, our objective must change from appeasing

Milosevic to sponsoring democratic change in Serbia and Milosevic's removal from power.

Democratic countries don't commit genocide and launch wars of aggression. But Milosevic's Serbia is not a democratic country. His ruthless power is maintained through fear and repression. He orchestrates attacks on academics, restricts freedom of assembly, maintains ironclad control on the judiciary, and harasses the media.

The Clinton people must stop trying to entice Milosevic and his cronies to dinners at French castles and instead treat him as the pariah that he is, while actively helping those in Serbia who oppose Milosevic's fascist regime and who understand that building a free, pluralistic society is the key to bringing down this bloody tyrant.

To this end, I am introducing legislation with Senators Richard Lugar, Gordon Smith, Joseph Lieberman, Frank Lautenberg, and others to make Milosevic's removal and Serbia's democratic transformation U.S. policy.

The bipartisan "Serbia Democratization Act" will, among other things:

- Authorize $100 million in U.S. funds to help support democracy and the development of a civil society inside Yugoslavia.

- Authorize increased Voice of America and Radio Free Europe/Radio Liberty broadcasting.

- Authorize assistance to victims of Milosevic's repression.

- Codify the "outer wall" of our sanctions on the Milosevic regime.

- Block all Yugoslav assets in the United States.

- Deny visas to senior Serbian and Yugoslav government officials.

- Require certification that Yugoslavia has a freely elected government before restoring Most Favored Nation trading status to Yugoslavia.

- Prohibit strategic exports and U.S. loans to Yugoslavia.

The goal of the legislation is to isolate Milosevic while at the same time engaging the Serb people and giving them resources with which to build democratic institutions and a pluralistic civil society.

The United States must work with democratic forces in Serbia to get out the message that it is Milosevic's autocratic rule and brutal repression in Kosovo that endangers Serbian territorial integrity. We must further make clear to the Serb people that a Yugoslavia whose government is based on democratic principles, the rule of law, and respect for human rights will be welcomed with open arms into the community of nations.

Milosevic's removal is our exit strategy, and it is the only policy that can bring lasting peace to the Balkans. The alternative is more indefinite and increasingly dangerous—U.S. military deployments in the Balkans.

Chapter 10
Cuba—
Castro's Tropical Gulag

THE QUESTION COMES UP AGAIN AND AGAIN: Why does Senator Helms care so much about a tiny communist island in the Caribbean? His answer is simple: "We become a part of what we condone." Trading with Castro would make us his accomplices in the oppression of the Cuban people.

Today, some in the American business community have launched an aggressive campaign against the Cuban embargo. They say that their agenda is not profit—that American investment would somehow help liberate the Cuban people.

In these essays, Senator Helms shows why they are wrong—dead wrong—and explains how to turn up the heat on, and get rid of, the last dictator in the Western Hemisphere.

TRADE WITH CASTRO? NO CIGAR
Cigar Aficionado, June 1999

PRESIDENT JOHN F. KENNEDY is said to have instructed his press secretary, Pierre Salinger, to go out one day and buy as many Cuban cigars as he could get his hands on. Salinger returned to the Oval Office the next day with more than a thousand Cuban cigars. President Kennedy, the story goes, inspected the loot and then took out his pen and signed the executive order imposing the Cuban embargo.

Kennedy may have been the last American to stock his humidor legally with Cuban tobacco, but in signing the Cuban embargo he did the right thing. And bipartisan majorities in both houses of Congress have supported the U.S. policy of isolating Castro's brutal dictatorship ever since.

In my Senate career, I've dedicated a great deal of my time and efforts to defending smokers' rights. But when it comes to Cuba, I put the human rights of the Cuban people far ahead of any smoker's right. We become a part of what we condone. And we Americans must never condone Castro's ruthless oppression of the Cuban people.

Castro is desperate for the United States to lift the embargo because he is desperate for hard currency to keep his faltering Marxist-Leninist economy afloat. For many years he was able to withstand the pressure of the U.S. embargo because the effects of the embargo were almost entirely offset by massive subsidies from the Soviet Union—upwards of $5 billion a year.

Only with the collapse of the Soviet Union in the 1990s has the embargo begun to have an effect, not only in Cuba but across the continent. The moment the embargo kicked in, Castro's efforts to finance Marxist insurgencies across Latin America stopped, allowing the nearly complete democratic transformation of the hemisphere.

Flooding Cuba now with new American investment and American tourists will do nothing to bring democracy to Cuba. To the contrary, it will give new life to Castro's crumbling regime. Here's why:

As almost any Cuban will confirm, the real cause of the misery of the Cuban people is not the U.S. embargo—it is Castro's

Marxist-Leninist economic system. Castro's Cuba is a brutal police state; Castro maintains power by fear, intimidation, and deprivation.

His regime controls every aspect of Cuban life—access to food, access to education, access to health care, and access to work. And if you say the wrong thing in Castro's tropical gulag, you lose your job. If you refuse to spy on your neighbor for the government, you don't get to go to college. If you dare to organize an opposition group, you go to jail.

American investment won't change this. It won't empower individual Cubans, nor will it give them independence from the regime. Why? Because foreign investors cannot do business with private Cuban citizens—they can go into business only with Castro.

Consider: It is illegal in Cuba for anyone except the regime to employ a Cuban citizen. Everyone works for Castro. Foreign investors can neither hire nor pay Cuban workers directly. They must pay Castro in hard currency for the workers. Castro then pays the workers in worthless Cuban pesos, while keeping the rest. Under these circumstances, American investment cannot help average Cubans—it would only help the Castro regime.

Consider a real-life example: Sheritt International is Canada's single largest investor in Cuba today. It is operating a stolen American-owned nickel mine at Moa Bay, where roughly one thousand Cubans work as virtual slave laborers. Sheritt pays Castro approximately $10,000 for each of those Cuban workers. Castro gives the workers the equivalent of about $18 a month in Cuban pesos—and then pockets the difference.

The result? Sheritt provides Castro with a $10 million direct cash subsidy each year. And what does Castro do with that hard currency infusion? He uses it to pay for his ruthless and cruel apparatus which keeps him in power—and the Cuban people in chains. Foreign investment can thus do nothing to promote

democracy, nothing to promote entrepreneurship or independence from the state. What it does is directly subsidize the
oppression of the Cuban people.

Tourism is another source of hard currency for the Castro
regime which Castro is desperately seeking to expand. Every one
of the tourist dollars spent in Cuba ends up in government
hands—the Cuban government owns all the hotels, and it owns all
the stores on the island.

And another side effect: Cuba has become the world's capital
of sex tourism. Thousands of destitute Cuban women, who cannot survive in Castro's Marxist-Leninist economy, have no choice
but to prostitute themselves with foreign tourists from Canada,
Italy, Germany, and other nations to get hard currency.

Many of these prostitutes—or *jinteras*—are schoolgirls as
young as twelve and thirteen. Others are educated women—doctors and lawyers—who cannot earn enough practicing their professions under Castro to feed their families. Americans simply
must not become a part of this degradation of Cuban women.

The United States must continue the embargo to keep up the
pressure for change on the island because if we don't give up our
leverage by unilaterally lifting the embargo, Castro's successors
will be forced to exchange normalized relations with the United
States for a complete democratic transition in Cuba.

Fidel Castro isn't going to live forever. He is going to leave
power in Cuba—either vertically or horizontally. And we need to
start planning for the day when he is no longer there as the uni-
fying force for tyranny on the island.

That is why maintaining the embargo, by itself, is not enough.
We need to start helping the Cuban people prepare for that day,
by helping them to create an independent civil society, helping
them to build free institutions, and getting resources to the

human rights advocates, independent journalists, and democracy activists so they can expand their space in society—just as Ronald Reagan helped the opposition leaders in Eastern Europe (who are now the presidents and prime ministers of free, democratic nations).

Last year, along with two dozen cosponsors, I proposed bipartisan legislation—the Cuban Solidarity Act—to provide $100 million over four years in humanitarian relief directly to the Cuban people through private charities on the island. We will pass it and send a message to Fidel Castro—and to the Cuban people—that Congress and the administration are united in our support for freedom in Cuba.

I look forward to the day when Americans can once again go to their corner stores and purchase Cuban cigars. But those cigars will have been produced by free labor in a free and democratic Cuba. To get to that day, we must keep the pressure on Castro, while simultaneously working to help the Cuban people build a free and independent civil society within the crumbling shell of Castro's teetering communist regime.

CUBANS MEET THEIR LIBERATOR
Miami Herald, January 23, 1998

IN THE OPENING SCENE of a 1970s documentary on the Cuban revolution, a young Fidel Castro is sitting around a campfire with his troops, recounting a story about taking on the Roman Catholic Church and "making a revolution against God."

Castro is telling his troops about a priest in Caracas (during South America's independence war) who was "inciting people"—

preaching against the revolution—when suddenly Simon Bolivar emerged from the throng. Castro says: "[Bolivar] takes his sword out and walks to the priest, climbs up on the altar, and belts him with the sword right across his back, knocking him down."

The soldiers cackle with laughter. The lesson, Castro says, is this: Bolivar "challenged the supernatural powers. He took the offensive."

Today, as Pope John Paul II tours Cuba, the tables are turned: The Catholic Church is the one taking the offensive. And Fidel Castro—the last remaining dictator in the Western Hemisphere—is about to be knocked down from the altar of his crumbling revolution.

In an ironic twist, the same Fidel Castro who fought the Catholic Church in his own "revolution against God" is turning to the leader of that church in a desperate bid for legitimacy. He invited John Paul to visit his tropical gulag in the misplaced hope that the pope's visit would strengthen Castro's grip on power. He plastered Havana with posters showing him shaking hands with the pope at the Vatican. He was counting on the pope to denounce the U.S. embargo and to join him in a condemnation of capitalist "materialism."

Castro has made a grave miscalculation. In John Paul, the Cuban people are meeting their liberator. No, Castro will not, under some papal spell, suddenly allow Cubans to choose their leaders in free elections. Cuba's political liberation will come in time. But today marks the moment of Cuba's spiritual liberation.

Spiritual liberation, the pope has demonstrated time and again, is the essential precursor to political liberation. With spiritual liberation comes the disappearance of fear. Cubans will hear the pope tell them over and over, in the same words that the risen Jesus told the apostles, "Be not afraid!" It is the maxim of his papacy.

Just as he has in each of his eighty other foreign trips, the pope will remind the Cuban people of their "inner freedom." He will tell them that, through their Christian faith, they already have been liberated—they are already free—because Christ has been sent for them, and all men, "to establish justice on the Earth...a light for the nations, to open the eyes of the blind, bring the prisoners from confinement, and, from the dungeon, those who live in darkness."

This message was the key to the pope's success in Poland. Following his 1979 visit there, a magical thing happened: Poles suddenly embraced this "inner freedom." They were no longer afraid. They began to behave like a free people, even though they were still enslaved. They began to speak more freely, associate more freely, and form independent institutions. Yes, there were crackdowns, but the process—once unleashed—proved unstoppable.

That process begins now in Cuba. A giant portrait of Jesus Christ has been raised in Cuba's "Revolution Square"—a place heretofore reserved for ideological rallies, military parades, and other displays of power by the Cuban Communist Party. A square that was built as a shrine to Castro's revolution will be transformed into a shrine of Christian faith.

And as Castro sits there, watching it all, I suspect that a creeping feeling of discomfort will come over him. It will be the same feeling that came over his former comrade, Edward Gierek of Poland, nineteen years ago, as this same pope said Mass in the center of Warsaw's Victory Square, and the Polish people began to chant, "We want God!"

Looking out over the throng, Castro will come to the sudden realization that a door has been opened in the hearts of the Cuban people—a door that he is powerless to shut.

REACHING OUT TO THE PEOPLE OF CUBA
A Radio Address on Cuba's *Radio Marti*, March 12, 1997

MY DEAR FRIENDS, in the year since the Libertad Act took effect, Fidel has told you a million lies about this law, which the U.S. Congress passed and President Clinton signed to support democracy and freedom in Cuba.

But here in America—where no dictator controls the news media and access to information—we know the truth. The law is working.

Fidel has reigned over you with an iron fist for nearly four decades, and for many of those long years, the world ignored your plight. No longer. Today, finally, the world is beginning to wake up and stand with you against Fidel. He is finally being recognized for what he is: a brutal, murderous despot, and the last remaining dictator in our hemisphere.

Fidel tells you that the world stands with him against the United States. He lies. Never has Castro been so isolated as he is today; never has he been so alone in the world.

One by one, the foreign investors who line Castro's pockets with money and keep his brutal regime afloat are fleeing. As each one leaves, the pressure builds on Fidel to loosen his stranglehold on Cuban society—to get out of your way and let you work, start businesses, earn a decent living, and feed your families.

And the governments of Europe and Latin America that once turned a blind eye to your oppression are finally joining the United States in pressing for human rights and democratic change in Cuba. Under pressure from the Libertad Act, the European Union has for the very first time adopted a "Common Position" on Cuba, committing Europe to press for the protection of human rights, reform of the criminal code, release of all political prisoners, an end to harassment of dissidents, and—yes—democracy.

Spain has stopped all nonhumanitarian aid to the Castro regime and has canceled Fidel's $15 million official credit line. In protest of Castro's tyranny, Nicaragua's newly elected president, Arnoldo Aleman, refused to invite Fidel to his inauguration. And the leaders of Chile, Argentina, El Salvador, Spain, and other Latin countries all stood together and made statements calling for change in Cuba—in front of Castro and the world—at the Ibero-American Summit in Santiago.

Yes, my friends, Fidel is alone—but you are not. More than ever before, the nations of the world are standing together with you. And at the same time that we here in Washington are building the pressure on Fidel to leave Cuba, we are preparing to help you rebuild once Castro does leave.

The Libertad Act requires that the U.S. government prepare a detailed plan for the economic aid and other assistance we will provide you to help rebuild in the wake of Castro's demise. Recently, the president of the United States unveiled that plan.

So, our message to you is: Your future once Fidel is gone is brighter than you can imagine. There will be investment, new jobs, freedom to start businesses, better housing, and a better life for all Cuban citizens. Your leaders will be chosen by you in free and democratic elections, and they will serve at your pleasure, not theirs.

And we in the United States will stand side by side with you and the leaders you choose, as friends, neighbors, and allies. And we will help you build a new Cuba, with jobs, prosperity, and opportunity for all.

My friends, soon Castro's tyranny will end. I look forward to the day when I can visit with you in a free, prosperous, and democratic Cuba. I am confident that day is not far off. *Libertad Para Cuba!*

ALLIES WITHOUT A MORAL COMPASS
Washington Times, July 19, 1996

SINCE THE PASSAGE OF THE HELMS-BURTON LAW, Canada, Mexico, and the European Union have bordered on apoplexy. Hysterical threats of "retaliatory measures" have poured forth from Ottawa and from the capitals of Europe and Latin America; protests have been lodged with international organizations; boycotts have been threatened.

Understandably, our friends in Canada, Europe, and Latin America feel that they have been slapped in the face—and indeed they have. But the slap did not come from Washington. It came from Havana.

Just weeks before the Helms-Burton bill became law, an interesting and little-noticed meeting took place in Havana. Spain's foreign minister at the time, Manuel Marin, traveled across the Atlantic for a ten-hour rendezvous with Cuban dictator Fidel Castro to open discussions on a new cooperative agreement between the European Union and Cuba.

In that meeting, Mr. Marin told Mr. Castro that his ability to deliver such an agreement would depend on Mr. Castro's willingness to ease up on dissidents, and he specifically brought up the Concilio Cubano, a new, national opposition movement. Mr. Marin held out the carrot of an agreement that represented potentially billions of dollars in new European investment on the island—if, that is, Mr. Castro moderated his behavior.

What was Mr. Castro's response? Within a few days, Castro—before Marin had even left Havana—had unleashed the largest and most brutal crackdown against dissidents on the island in more than a decade, rounding up more than two hundred dissidents associated with Concilio Cubano.

A week later, with that crackdown still in full swing, Mr. Castro ordered his Soviet MiG fighter jets into the air to shoot down two unarmed American civilian aircraft flying in international airspace, murdering four innocent human beings in cold blood.

Since then two things have happened. The U.S. Congress passed and President Clinton signed into law the Helms-Burton (or Libertad) Act. And the European Union quietly shelved its plans for a cooperative agreement with Mr. Castro.

Our friends in Europe might prefer to forget this chain of events, but they had better keep it in mind if they intend to pursue their challenges to the Helms-Burton law. For these events not only precipitated the passage of that law, they totally and completely discredited their policies of economic engagement with the Castro regime.

For years, Europe, Canada, and others have tried to justify their shameful trade with Cuba by explaining that they are not really profiteering from tyranny and that their investment "gives them influence with Castro," enabling them to nudge Mr. Castro toward respecting human rights and behaving like a member of the community of civilized nations.

Cuba's recent actions have given the lie to those moralistic pretensions. Faced with the choice between a new and profitable trade agreement with Europe and restraint in his behavior toward the democratic opposition of the island, Mr. Castro told Europe, in effect, to keep its money.

Sooner or later, our friends are going to have to face an uncomfortable fact: Their policies in Cuba have failed. Despite a near flood of deutsche marks, dollars, pounds, pesos, and francs into the Cuban government's coffers, Mr. Castro has not—and will not—reform. Those who try to justify their investments in Cuba by cloaking them in specious arguments are fooling nobody but themselves. Their investment in Cuba does nothing to help the Cuban people. To the contrary, they are helping keep Mr. Castro in power.

When European or Canadian companies invest in Cuba, they do not work with private businessmen—they enter into joint ventures with the Cuban government. They do not go out and hire workers, providing hard currency the workers can use to feed their families. Each company is required to pay Mr. Castro a substantial sum—as much as $10,000 for each worker—and Mr. Castro in turn pays that worker several hundred Cuban pesos, a fraction of the original amount. The regime pockets the difference.

This is not empowerment of the Cuban people—it is taking advantage of what amounts to slave labor. All the same, this is precisely why some foreign businesses are so upset with the Libertad Act: Cuba, with its cheap slave labor, is a paradise for investors with no moral compass. Ethically bankrupt investors are the obvious linchpin holding together Mr. Castro's faltering dictatorship.

Since losing his previous $5 billion to $6 billion in annual Soviet subsidies, Mr. Castro has been frantically seeking to capitalize on property stolen from American citizens to finance his crumbling regime. And he has found many British, Canadian, French, Mexican, and other foreign accomplices willing to traffic in this stolen property.

This point is conveniently ignored by governments complaining about the Helms-Burton law—it affects only those foreign companies who trade in stolen American property. These "investors" do not differ morally from common street criminals, who trade in stolen goods like cars and stereos. The difference is that these executives do their trafficking on Lear jets instead of in seedy chop shops on the bad side of town.

If they were doing domestically what they are doing internationally—trading in stolen goods—they'd face prosecution and, most likely, jail terms. Instead, they enjoy the protection of their governments, whose leaders stand up before the world and defend the indefensible with unworthy indignation.

This deliberate, knowing trade in stolen American property is about to come to an end. The Libertad Act puts these accomplices to Mr. Castro's property thefts on notice that if they enrich themselves with property pilfered from American citizens, they will be persona non grata in the United States, and they will be held liable by the legitimate American owners.

So this is why Title III of the Libertad Act is enormously important. By creating a private right of action allowing Americans to sue these traffickers for compensation, it will put an end to this illegal trade in stolen property. President Clinton's shameful decision to suspend this provision for six months merely delays the inevitable. The threat of lawsuits still hangs over the necks of Mr. Castro's business partners like the blade of a guillotine. And sooner or later, that blade will fall.

It is time that our European, Canadian, and Latin American allies cease lashing out at the United States and take a good hard look in the mirror. They should be honest with themselves: Their trade with Mr. Castro is doing nothing to bring about democracy or protect human rights in Cuba.

It is my sincere hope that once Canada and the European Union get over their injured innocence and look objectively at the events that hastened the enactment of the Helms-Burton law, they will see that their trade with Mr. Castro has not moderated his behavior one iota. He is still the arrogant, brutal dictator he was thirty years ago. Any impartial observer will testify that the European policy of collaboration with Mr. Castro is a miserable failure. It is time for them to join the U.S. embargo and isolate Mr. Castro's despicable regime.

At a minimum, those who do business with this communist dictator should acknowledge to the world that they are cashing in on the misery of the Cuban people. Furthermore, these traffickers should muster the decency to cease their accusations that the United States is somehow a bad neighbor and ally. It is they who are the bad neighbors and who deserve neither sympathy nor respect.

TOURISTS WON'T LIBERATE CUBA
USA Today, January 9, 1996

I DON'T DOUBT THE SINCERITY of those who assert that an invasion of American tourists would be the straw that broke the back of Fidel Castro's tyranny. However, such arguments are sincerely wrong.

In fact, the opposite is true. Castro hopes the United States will lift the travel ban for the same reason he wants the trade embargo lifted: He is desperate for hard currency to keep his faltering regime afloat.

We must not give it to him. Flooding Cuba with American tourists would do nothing to bring democracy to Cuba. For years Castro has lured cash-bearing Europeans, Canadians, Mexicans, and others to Cuba, yet his regime remains one of the most oppressive on earth. Adding Americans to that mix would only prolong the misery of the Cuban people.

Tourism is a principal source of hard currency that Castro is desperate to expand. Cuba's state economic sector is collapsing.

Last summer the regime announced layoffs for 400,000 workers, ending the revolution's promise of universal employment. This forebodes an economic crisis even Castro will be unable to explain or ignore, one that must not be swept away by an influx of American tourist dollars. The real cause of Cuba's economic crisis is Castro's refusal to give up his monopoly over Cuban economic life.

American tourism would simply subsidize Cuba's despotic government. It would not permit Cubans to own businesses or enjoy the fruits of their own labor. Under Castro's dictatorship, it is a crime to operate most forms of private business or for one Cuban to employ another.

Worse, existing foreign tourism has turned Cuba into what one Italian magazine called a "paradise of sexual tourism." Thousands of Cuban women prostitute themselves with foreign visitors for hard currency. Castro allows these women no other way to feed themselves or their families. Many are children as young as twelve or thirteen; others are educated women, doctors and lawyers, who cannot subsist in Castro's Cuba practicing their professions.

Americans cannot avoid becoming a part of what they condone. We simply must not become part of this degradation of Cuban women by condoning Castro's cruelty. We must do nothing to prolong the suffering for so long imposed on the Cuban people. Lifting the travel ban would do exactly that. It would supply Castro with the hard currency he needs to stay in power while doing absolutely nothing to improve the lives of the Cuban people. Lifting the travel ban would be immoral and unprincipled. We must not do it.

CASTRO BLOWS A GASKET
USA Today, June 14, 1995

THERE HAS BEEN AN UNPRECEDENTED hue and cry in Havana since I introduced the "Cuban Liberty and Democratic Solidarity Act." Fidel Castro has screamed that I am a "crazy man," a "fascist," and compared me to Hitler. Meanwhile, Castro's chief lieutenant, National Assembly president Ricardo Alarcon, has called my bill "the plan of a madman," an "annexationist monster," and an "attempt to recolonize Cuba." They have launched what they hope will be an international campaign to defeat the bill; they've even threatened to unleash a new wave of refugees if it is passed by the U.S. Congress.

Obviously, I have struck a nerve.

The reaction of Castro and his cronies is highly instructive. Those in the United States who suggest the United States should end sanctions and normalize relations with Castro are making the puzzling argument that allowing American investment in Cuba is the best way to undermine his regime. If that is indeed the case, then why is Castro so desperate for the United States to lift the embargo? And why is he so afraid of my bill?

The answer is obvious: The embargo is working. My bill will tighten it and deny Castro the two things he most desperately wants: international legitimacy and U.S. hard currency. More than anything, Castro wants to end his pariah status in the world. With the end of the Cold War and the defeat of the Soviet empire, Castro is the hemisphere's odd man out—a retrograde communist in a world of free markets and free societies. He desperately wants international legitimacy.

His yearning for legitimacy is precisely why Castro jumped at the opportunity to sign the refugee repatriation agreement with the United States. The agreement sends a message to the world that the United States trusts Castro and considers him someone we can work with. After all, if U.S. ships can dock in Havana harbor and hand fleeing Cubans over to Castro, how bad can he really be?

The agreement allows Cuban officials to hold high-level, direct negotiations with senior American officials, imputing a false legitimacy to Castro, and it has opened new and senior channels of communication between our countries.

What did Castro give up for all of this? Nothing, except a promise not to launch a new wave of refugees upon our shores. The fact is, Castro sees this agreement as an opening—a chance to begin normalizing relations without giving up control. My bill, by contrast, makes it clear that the only path to normalization is the removal of Castro from power.

Castro is also desperate for hard currency. For three decades, American isolation of Castro was offset by generous subsidies from the USSR—around $5 billion annually. Today, those subsidies are gone, and for the very first time U.S. sanctions are hitting hard.

As the Cuban economy slips further and further into depression, Castro is feeling the pressure of the embargo as never before. He recently announced that Havana will for the first time lay off some 400,000 workers, ending the revolution's promise of universal employment. Faced with almost a half million unemployed workers, the Cuban government is now being forced to confront the question of whether to allow self-employment and the creation of some private businesses—i.e., giving up its monopoly over Cuban economic life and its role as the country's sole employer.

Lifting the embargo would lift this pressure on the Castro regime by unleashing a flood of hard currency into Cuba—hard currency that would go directly into Cuban government coffers and would allow it to put off the day of reckoning.

Sadly, some in the United States want to let up the pressure by allowing corporate America to replace Soviet Russia as Castro's benefactor. That is exactly what Castro wants because it would allow him to avoid confronting the failures of his centrally controlled economy.

The United States must never compromise its principles. We must not play by Castro's rules. We must not relieve him of the pressure of the embargo by giving him the undeserved legitimacy and hard currency he so desperately desires. If Castro wants us to lift the embargo, we must move in the opposite direction. We must increase the pressure. And that is exactly what my bill will do.

The Libertad Act will cut off Castro's lifeline of hard currency and increase his pariah status within the international community. It makes clear that only a democratically elected Cuban government will receive the benefits of American trade and recognition. And, in light of the administration's decision to work with Cuba to repatriate refugees fleeing Castro's tropical gulag, it reasserts that U.S. policy is to isolate, not cooperate with, Castro's despotic regime.

Those tempted by the siren call of normalization should look at the issue from Castro's perspective. What kind of policy would he have the United States adopt to ensure he remains in power? He wants an influx of American hard currency and increased trade and legitimacy from the United States. What he does not want is for the "Cuban Liberty and Democratic Solidarity Act" to become law, which is the best reason I can think of to pass it.

WHY HELMS-BURTON?
Washington Post, May 4, 1995

THE *WASHINGTON POST*'S EDITORIAL PAGES have bristled with pious outrage since the introduction of the "Cuban Liberty and Democratic Solidarity Act." Surprisingly raw nerves have been touched, prompting a somewhat hysterical demand that U.S. policy toward Cuba now strengthen Fidel Castro's bloody hand.

Some who favor doing away with sanctions altogether have reacted with a puzzling degree of self-righteousness. Ignore, they say in effect, the cruel and bloody tyranny that Castro has inflicted for so long upon the Cuban people.

Strange to say, the Clinton administration appears to be attentive to blandishments that "now is the time" to begin taking "calibrated steps" toward full recognition of a communist regime that a series of U.S. presidents condemned for nightmarish human rights violations.

President Clinton would do well to think twice before he agrees to end the thirty-year bipartisan U.S. policy of isolating the Castro dictatorship. If Clinton wants to ensure Castro's survival—and the continued suffering of the Cuban people—he should bow to those advising him to hoist the white flag of surrender. The administration's announcement Tuesday that the United States will hereafter cooperate with Castro's brutal security apparatus (to capture Cubans fleeing Castro's repression and turn them over to his thugs in Havana) is seen by many as the first of these "calibrated steps."

Ending the embargo would play right into Castro's hands. Castro wants sanctions lifted because doing business with America would, among other things, legitimize his communist dictatorship. It would inject life (and hard currency) into Cuba's moribund state-run economy. It would remove popular pressure on his brutal regime.

Most of those who advocate lifting the sanctions are longtime Castrophiles, joined recently by certain libertarian conservatives who argue that allowing American companies to do business with Castro would help undermine his regime by unleashing the power of the free market in Cuba.

That scenario may sound good, but behind the facade is snake oil. Castro's Cuba is a statist, socialist economy that has taken no significant steps toward liberalization. Thus, it remains an arrestable offense for Cuban citizens to operate almost any form of private business. Cubans are arrested regularly for trying to scrape together a living by acting as entrepreneurs: using their cars as private taxis, running private restaurants out of their homes, or selling cakes and coffee to farmers. Lifting sanctions would do nothing to help these oppressed people.

What it would assuredly do is allow American companies to conduct joint ventures with Cuba's state-owned enterprises. And just whom would this help? It would help Castro, by bailing out his bankrupt regime and delivering scarce dollars to his coffers; it would to nothing to promote economic opportunity or political freedom for most Cubans.

Opponents of the embargo argue that lifting sanctions and making concessions to Castro would encourage him to make free-market and democratic reforms. Talk about nonsense! Castro reads the newspapers. He has surely pondered the fate of other communist leaders who have enacted reforms—Gorbachev in Russia, Jaruzelski in Poland, Ceauçescu in Romania—only to lose power (and in some cases their lives). He has no intention of traveling down that path of his own free will.

Castro needs a final push. My bill will provide it, by tightening existing sanctions against Castro while making it clear that the United States will do everything in its power to terminate his brutal dictatorship. Among other things, this legislation will:

• Require the president to seek an international embargo of the Castro dictatorship in the UN Security Council.

• Strengthen U.S. broadcasting into Cuba.

- Prohibit importation into the United States of sugar, syrups, or molasses from any country that imports Cuban sugar.

- Deny entry into the United States of anyone who has benefited from U.S. property confiscated by Castro.

- Prohibit any loans, credits, or financing to any such person or agency.

- Create a right of action in U.S. courts for any American citizen who has had property confiscated against anyone who has purchased, trafficked in, or benefited from that property.

In short, the goal of S.381 is to protect the rights of American citizens, cut off Castro's lifeline of hard currency, and send this clear and unmistakable message to foreign businessmen: If you want to do business in the Cuban and American economies, you have to make a choice. And, just as important, the bill instructs the president to begin preparing the United States for dealing with a post-Castro Cuba and gives him predetermined authority to help a democratically elected Cuban government get on its feet and begin rebuilding the island.

If Castro has survived sanctions for three decades, my detractors ask, why tighten sanctions now? The answer is obvious: For the first time in three decades, sanctions finally have a chance of working. During the Cold War, Cuba enjoyed generous subsidies from Moscow, which propped up Castro's regime by offsetting any pressure created by the embargo. Now that the Cold War has ended, so have the subsidies. Sanctions can now, at long last, have their intended effect.

Now is the time to tighten the screws, not loosen them. And now is the time for the Clinton administration to stop playing footsie with the forces of capitulation and support this act.

Chapter 11

The Middle East

THE UNITED STATES HAS ONLY one true friend and ally in the Middle East—Israel. There are others nations with which we trade, some which we defend, and some who even share our interests. But none of these is, as Senator Helms has said on many occasions, like Israel: the equivalent of an American carrier battle group in the region.

Senator Helms has always insisted that the United States formulate its foreign policy with an eye to our own interests in the world. The subjugation of all U.S. interests in the Middle East to the peace process has effectively meant that terrorism goes unpunished, that dictatorship flourishes without opposition, and that groups with American blood on their hands become "partners" in peace.

In these articles, written for *The Weekly Standard* and *USA Today*, Senator Helms makes the case that until the United States promotes freedom and democracy—eschewing the usual wink and nod to the Assads and Arafats of the world—there will be no lasting peace for the Middle East.

HAFEZ AL-ASSAD, MURDERER
The Weekly Standard, June 26, 2000

HAFEZ AL-ASSAD WAS NOT A DIPLOMAT, he was not a peacemaker, he was not a great leader. He was a murderer. In his three decades in power, the Syrian dictator terrorized his own nation, the people of Lebanon, and countless others.

President Clinton bowed his head and bit his lower lip upon receiving the news of Assad's death; it almost seemed that a tear might creep down his cheek. And, in a sign of misplaced respect, the president sent Secretary of State Madeleine Albright to represent him at Assad's funeral. Albright herself eulogized Assad as a "major figure" and expressed sadness at his passing.

There is no justification for honoring a man like Assad. He is a leader on a par in cruelty with Saddam Hussein. In 1982, after a minor rebellion broke out in the city of Hama, Assad sent in his troops (under the command of his brother) and brutally murdered twenty thousand innocent people. The Syrian people live in fear, afraid to speak out, afraid to demand basic human rights and political freedoms. Assad, in short, was a man to be reviled.

Yes, it is true that rural Syria now has electricity and that under the Assad regime the Syrian people have not been troubled by successive coups. But the Syrian people also live under the thumb of no less than fifteen internal "security" agencies, which regulate their lives and suppress their rights to free speech and free association. Fax machines are heavily regulated; cellular communications and the Internet are reserved for a few chosen elites.

Assad left the Syrian people impoverished because he feared economic freedom would undermine his dictatorship. Small business can barely operate because there is no private banking. A nation known for its merchant class is mired in deep poverty. Small things that make daily life bearable—decent roads, buildings, and communications—are nonexistent.

There is also the pathetic tale of Lebanon. Invited in by Lebanon's Christian leadership in 1976, Assad quickly turned on his hosts. Syrian troops still occupy Lebanon twenty-four years later.

The Lebanese people are cowed by decades of Syrian-sponsored communal wars; Lebanese leaders are bereft of national pride to the point that they predicate their own peace and security with Israel on an Israeli withdrawal from the once-Syrian Golan Heights!

And what of Assad's celebrated commitment to peace—his "strategic choice" in the words of President Clinton and the secretary of state? Who is this man of peace? He is a state sponsor of terrorism, who went to his grave with the blood of Americans on his hands.

Assad was almost certainly involved in the bombing of the U.S. Marine barracks in Beirut in 1983, which left 241 American servicemen dead. He supported Palestinian terrorists, Kurdish terrorists, Irish terrorists, and Japanese terrorists. Syria is to this day the main conduit through which the odious Hezbollah gets its weapons.

Notwithstanding the continued operation of Hezbollah; notwithstanding the continued sanctuary Assad provided for rejectionist Palestinian terrorist groups in Damascus; notwithstanding Syria's continued intransigence on peace in the face of almost unimaginable concessions by the government of Israel, the Clinton administration continued to swear by Assad. The fact that Assad chose a meeting with President Clinton earlier this year to reject yet another offer of peace with Israel—a slap in the face to the United States government—seems not to faze administration officials one bit.

Assad is dead, and his son Bashar has been installed (for the moment) as the new Syrian dictator. The Russians, once Syria's best ally, did not send a government representative to his funeral; nor did the Chinese, Syria's main arms supplier. But for the funeral of this state sponsor of terrorism, this murderer, President Clinton sent his secretary of state. For shame.

Rather than bowing before Assad's casket, the United States should be delivering a clear message of solidarity to the people of Syria: You did not deserve a dictator like Assad. You deserve peace with your neighbor, Israel. You deserve the freedom to hold elections and to choose your own leaders. You deserve a better life. Now is the time to grab it. We stand with you in the hope that the end of Hafez al-Assad will mean the beginning of freedom for Syria.

MIDDLE EAST BLACKMAIL
USA Today, April 14, 1997

IN THE PAST MONTH, YASSER ARAFAT has led a terrorist Palestinian group to assume it has his approval for acts of terrorism against Israel. He has urged the Arab League to resume its boycott of Israel. As a result, the peace process has plummeted to its lowest ebb in recent memory.

The behavior of Arafat and his cohorts has reduced the "peace process" to scarcely more than blackmail. The Palestinians and their Arab partners have formulated a dangerous either/or threat: Peace on their terms or suffer their boycotts, bombs, and stones. All of this seems to be based on the weird presumption that it will have no impact on relations with the United States.

This presumption is terribly wrong. For years it has been obvious that certain realities have been unclear to the Arab parties to the peace process. The Department of State, constrained by the meaningless rhetoric of diplomacy, is ill equipped to convey those very clear realities. It is long past time that Arafat and company wake up and smell the coffee.

The American people are not likely to be bullied away from their friendship and support for the state of Israel. Americans want a foreign policy dictated by values, not by realpolitik.

They respect democracy, and they like Israel because they feel comfortable with a system of majority rule, of elections, of civil and political freedom.

Congress needs no pro-Israel lobby to instruct us as to why we should support Israel. The United States cares about Israel because the values held dear by Americans are reflected in Israel. Those who undertake to subvert these values earn our enmity. We should not engage with them; we should not trade with them; we must do our utmost to isolate them. (Witness U.S. policies against Iran and Cuba.)

The Palestinians, led by Arafat, have labored too long under the delusion that because they are engaged in an illusory, on-again, off-again peace process with Israel, they have no obligation to abide by the standards expected of other nations in partnership with the United States. The Palestinians must understand the choice confronting them: They can adopt our values, reject further terrorism, and embrace democracy; or they can join the pariahs.

For other participants in the Arab League's recent hate fest in Cairo, similar conditions apply. There are indeed relationships with many Arab states that are important to us. But if they undertake to revert to the old boycott days, there are U.S. laws to restrict the scope of our relations, and they will be applied.

These realities must be made completely clear throughout the Middle East, especially in light of the impending final status talks between Israel and the Palestinians. There is little doubt that once the peace process clears this current hurdle, discussions of the ultimate disposition of the West Bank and Jerusalem can and will commence. On this, the views of the Congress are clear:

Jerusalem is the united capital of the state of Israel, and the United States will support its remaining so forever. If this is unacceptable to the Arab parties to the peace process and if they resort to terrorism, boycotts, and other failed policies of the past, relations with the United States will surely deteriorate.

America's acceptance of the Palestine Liberation Organization (PLO) as a negotiating party in the peace process became possible conditioned on the PLO's decision to renounce terrorism. For those willing to embrace the fantasy that terrorists are, somehow, freedom fighters, the PLO's words alone were enough. For the rest of us, renunciation of terrorism demands that Arafat and the Palestinian Authority must not merely condemn acts of terror but must also actively prevent such acts and imprison the perpetrators.

I confess a lack of interest in the exigencies of Palestinian balance of power politics that "require" Arafat to entertain Hamas and Islamic Jihad.

If, during the final status talks, we are obliged to look forward to PLO-sanctioned acts of terrorism and a chorus of threats from the Arab League, Israel and its friend will have little incentive to attend such talks. That would not, of course, reflect any change in America's relationship with Israel, which is based on shared values. But it will bode ill for the U.S.-Palestinian relationship, which, after all, is based on the peace process and little else.

Chapter 12
Haitian "Democracy"

THE CLINTON ADMINISTRATION HAS OFTEN pointed to its invasion to "restore democracy" in Haiti as one of the administration's greatest foreign policy achievements. As Senator Helms demonstrates here, it was nothing of the sort.

From 1991 to 1994, Haiti was run by a violent military regime that came to power in a coup against the elected president, Jean-Bertrand Aristide. Elected or not, Aristide was a demagogue who used his position of power to strike out against his opponents and feed the fires of class warfare.

As chairman of the Foreign Relations Committee, Senator Helms has resisted the Clinton administration's efforts to sidle up to the obviously anti-American Aristide and has sought to expose the anti-democratic actions, narco-corruption, and political murders associated with Aristide and his inner circle.

In this essay, Senator Helms chronicles the missteps and miscalculations of the Clinton administration's policy in Haiti and its dire consequences for the democracy movement in Haiti. It is not just a postmortem on a failed policy—it is a message to Haitian authorities that the era of blind U.S. support for their regime is ending.

LETTING ARISTIDE GET AWAY WITH MURDER
Miami Herald, October 20, 2000

CONSTITUTIONAL ORDER: SUSPENDED.

Government institutions: dysfunctional.

Political murderers: on the loose.

Law and order: disintegrating.

Elections: fraudulent.

Drug smuggling: rampant.

Four years after Vice President Gore proclaimed the Clinton administration's Haiti policy as "one of the most deft uses of diplomacy and military force in combination that you will find anywhere in the annals of the history of this country," it is today little more than the smoldering wreckage of a wrongheaded policy. (Responsibility for these disastrous results rests squarely with cynical, inept policymakers in the White House.)

Haiti scarcely would be a priority for the United States had the Clinton-Gore administration not used the full measure of U.S. power and influence to restore President Jean-Bertrand Aristide to power five years ago. Certainly, the Haitians have done their part to waste the opportunities given them by U.S. taxpayers (and twenty thousand U.S. troops). The spoilers were, by great irony, the very people President Clinton restored to power: Aristide and his entourage of thugs.

Prior to invading Haiti, the administration refused to acknowledge the obvious realities: (1) There was no record of democracy upon which to build, and (2) Aristide was neither a democrat nor a friend. Nevertheless, the administration centered its policy on the restoration of Aristide, not democracy.

Taking his side and his puppet successor's, the Clinton-Gore administration ignored the democratic opposition, shunned Haiti's pluralistic parliament, and let Aristide's cohorts literally get away with murder. It worked only half-heartedly with the legislature and opposition parties and then under pressure from the U.S. Congress. And, by tolerating a series of farcical elections, the administration is set to deliver Haiti directly into the hands of Aristide and his thuggish associates in national elections by year's end.

The Clinton administration has wasted more than $30 million on a succession of flawed and fraudulent elections. Instead of acknowledging and fixing problems, the administration and biased OAS observer missions pushed Haitians to settle for farcical processes, discrediting democracy itself.

By the 1997 legislative elections, Haitians had become so disillusioned that voter participation dwindled to less than 5 percent. With declining participation came greater consolidation of power in the hands of Aristide's cultish Lavalas movement.

Despite a lead-up to the May 2000 elections characterized by President René Preval's antidemocratic maneuvering, violence, stolen election materials, and logistical difficulties, many Haitians voted courageously in local and legislative elections. Unwilling to share power, the ruling Lavalas Party pressured the electoral council to certify false results and drove the president of the council to refuge in the United States. With him out of the way, fraudulent results became the official results.

There is also a depressing irony that the Clinton administration, which used human rights violations to justify the invasion policy, maintained the mere appearance of human rights monitoring in Haiti.

Today, Preval's government continues to block investigations into political murders. Impunity prevails.

Although the Clinton administration often has touted the creation of the Haitian National Police as the cornerstone of law and order in Haiti, it has dropped the ball there as well. The police force has come under relentless attacks. Added to this is the erosion of the police force by corruption, politicization, drug trafficking, and human rights violations.

Also, in five years of U.S. stewardship, Haiti has become a primary transit point for cocaine bound for the United States and has done so poorly on drug cooperation that it has been twice "decertified" by Clinton.

Last year, then–U.S. ambassador to Haiti Timothy Carney noted: "Haiti is a long way from getting democracy. It lacks nearly all of the elements that make up a democracy. Overall, our expectations were too high. Did we let ourselves be led by our hopes instead of analysis?"

The answer is yes.

Misguided hopes aside, consider what could have been done—in flood-ravaged North Carolina, for example—with a fraction of the $3 billion frittered away by an irresponsible administration on an unreliable partner in Haiti.

The White House probably never will admit to itself that its "success" in Haiti was never more than a fiction sustained at the expense of U.S. credibility, the military, the taxpayers, and the aspirations of the Haitian people.

The rest of us know the awful truth.

Chapter 13
The War on Drugs

COLOMBIA IS THE SOURCE OF 80 PERCENT of the cocaine that enters America's streets and schoolyards. For this reason, Senator Helms has made the fight against narco-corruption in Colombia one of his most important missions in the U.S. Senate.

When Senator Helms assumed the chairmanship of the Foreign Relations Committee, Colombia was being run by a president, Ernesto Samper, who had been elected with millions in contributions from Colombian drug traffickers. He was turning Colombia into what Helms called a "narco-democracy." Senator Helms was determined to ensure that Samper was removed from power, by making Colombia a pariah state, ostracized from the international community, so long as its president was in the pocket of the drug kingpins.

In these essays, Senator Helms chronicles the battle for Colombia—first the successful battle to oust the narco-corrupt President Samper and then against Colombia's "narco-guerrillas" who today threaten to overrun the reform government of Samper's successor, Andres Pastrana, and establish a narco-dictatorship in Colombia. In the results of this battle to stem the tide of Colombian drug trafficking lies the fate of millions of American children.

COLOMBIA: AMERICA'S FAVORITE
NARCO-DEMOCRACY
Wall Street Journal, April 4, 1995
(with William J. Bennett)

THE DELUGE OF ILLEGAL DRUGS flooding into the United States has become one of the principal threats to our national security. More Americans die each year from the use of cocaine, heroin, and other illegal drugs than from international terrorism. Yet, while the Clinton administration has rightly maintained a tough line with Libya, Iran, and other governments known to be sponsoring terrorism, it has let Colombia—which ships more cocaine into the United States than any other country—completely off the hook. It is time for the administration to stiffen its spine and show some resolve in its antidrug efforts.

The administration's recent annual review of international cooperation on counterdrug efforts by major drug-producing and -trafficking countries is instructive. Under this review, countries that fail to meet certain minimum standards of performance in combating drug trafficking are supposed to be denied American aid. The Clinton administration acknowledged in its report that Colombia has received a "national interest waiver," allowing American aid to flow into Colombia despite its miserable record.

This is a grave moral and geopolitical mistake. All available evidence clearly indicates Colombia has totally capitulated to the drug lords. By extending certification to Colombia, despite overwhelming evidence that its government is rife with narco-corruption, the Clinton administration has sent a troubling signal to all drug-producing nations: The United States will impose no penalty for collusion in trafficking with the drug lords.

Colombia is no borderline case. It has indisputably become a "narco-democracy"—a country with a facade of democratic government that is effectively controlled by drug kingpins who manipulate the political establishment with cocaine money. According to the administration's own background papers on Colombia:

- The Cali cartel has been left free by the Colombian government to exploit the banking system and launder vast sums of drug money with impunity.

- There is practically no effective investigation or prosecution of the more than fifteen thousand current cases of corruption involving government officials (more than half of them senior-level authorities).

- A "guilt-laundering" system exists, in which Cali drug lords surrender and submit to a jury-rigged plea-bargaining system that leaves their assets intact and allows them to plead to minor charges.

- The government's eradication programs have been half-hearted at best, despite massive increases in the growing of opium and cocaine cultivation.

- High-level government collusion enables the shipment of enormous quantities of cocaine into the United States, with 727 jets transiting in Mexico with tons of the drug.

- There is evidence of the corruption of many members of the Colombian Congress and increasing evidence of presidential ties to the drug cartels.

The Clinton administration cannot plead ignorance as the excuse for its abdication of responsibility. But conditions in Colombia are in fact worse than even the administration's report acknowledges. The influence of the cartels and their blood money pervades almost all aspects of Colombia's political, social, and economic life. Cartel money finances political campaigns. It silences journalists. It buys judges. It infiltrates virtually every major business activity in Colombia—from cut flowers, to oil, to paper, to banking.

Colombia is now the primary base for the cartels to extend their drug operations throughout the hemisphere. Despite the fact that the Cali cartel now supplies more than 80 percent of all the cocaine entering the United States, the Colombian government has failed to arrest or prosecute even one significant cartel member. To the contrary, Colombia has given the cartel cover and protection from international extradition, allowing these drugs to end up on American streets and in American schools, where they destroy the lives of American children.

We believe the Colombian government's collusion with the drug lords poses a direct threat to the national security of the United States. It is time to meet this threat head-on. And since the Clinton administration has failed to provide leadership on this issue, it is all the more important that Congress assume responsibility. That is why a Senate Foreign Relations subcommittee will hold a hearing today on the issue—and why legislation will be introduced this week to cut off all economic support, trade benefits, and military assistance to Colombia by February 6, 1996, unless the president of the United States can certify that Colombian president Ernesto Samper has implemented the reform agenda he promised the U.S. Congress he would enact.

Elements of this agenda include investigating the financing by drug traffickers of political parties and candidates in Colombia;

putting law enforcement resources behind investigating, capturing, convicting, and imprisoning major drug lords in Colombia; ending the "guilt-laundering" system; confiscating assets of cartel leaders; and destroying 41,000 hectares (108,680 acres) of coca and poppy plants in Colombia by January 1, 1996 (and all remaining acreage by January 1, 1997).

The Colombian leaders must be sent a clear and unmistakable message: In the war on drugs, they can either continue to ally themselves with the cartels, and thereby become a pariah state like Libya and Iran, or return to the community of civilized nations, fulfill the promises President Samper made, and join with the United States in an effort to put the cartels out of business. The choice is theirs.

THE CHALLENGE TO COLOMBIA
Wall Street Journal, March 4, 1996

LAST YEAR, FORMER DRUG CZAR WILLIAM BENNETT and I warned that Colombia was degenerating into a "narco-democracy," and I challenged Colombian president Ernesto Samper to make a choice: Enter into an alliance with the drug cartels and turn Colombia into a pariah state like Iran and Libya, or join the community of civilized nations in a campaign to put the drug cartels out of business.

What we did not know at the time of last year's writing was that President Samper had already made his choice: He sided with the cartels.

In the past year, overwhelming evidence has emerged that Mr. Samper knowingly accepted more than $6 million in campaign contributions from the leaders of the Cali drug cartel. The charge was leveled by no less than Mr. Samper's closest friend and political ally, former defense minister and campaign chairman Fernando Botero. Evidence of his collusion with the drug traffickers has now been presented to the Colombian Congress by Colombia's chief prosecutor, the able and honest Alfonso Valdivieso.

Mr. Samper made his choice. Last week came time for the United States to respond. After months of congressional pressure, and faced with an avalanche of evidence, President Clinton had no choice but to "decertify" Colombia, labeling it a country in non-compliance with U.S. narcotics policy. The president leveled the requisite sanctions against Mr. Samper's narco-corrupted government for its complicity in the poisoning of millions of Americans with deadly narcotics.

Last year, President Clinton had granted Colombia a "national interest waiver," acknowledging that Colombia's performance in the drug war was unacceptable but imposing no penalty for its failure to perform. This was a mistake. Waiving the law again would have made a mockery of our commitment to halt the flood of illegal drugs from Colombia and would have set back the efforts of those in Colombia working at great personal risk to clean up the system.

President Clinton has finally joined Congress in sending a strong (and now unified) message to Mr. Samper and his cronies that his collusion with drug traffickers is unacceptable. Now the challenge is for the Colombian people to rid their system of narco-corruption and save their democracy. Colombians are justifiably proud of their democracy, but it has in recent years been riddled from top to bottom with the corrupting influence of drug money. Colombia's political, judicial, law enforcement, and military structures are all mired in drug corruption. Large contributions have been given by Cali cartel leaders not only to President Samper but also to Colombian congressmen, senators, and senior executive branch officials, including the attorney general.

This narco-corruption is a threat to both the rule of law in Colombia and to the vital national interests of the United States. Just as the cartels are poisoning Colombia's democracy, so too are they poisoning our schools, our streets, and our children. The Colombian cartels—principally the Cali and Valle del Cauca cartels—are responsible for 80 percent of the cocaine and 30 percent of the heroin entering the United States today. While exact statistics do not exist, Drug Enforcement Agency officials estimate that these operations produced more than seven hundred metric tons of cocaine in 1994, yielding more than $7 billion in U.S. sales alone.

The human and financial costs for the United States of this influx of lethal narcotics are enormous. Last year alone, drug consumption cost American taxpayers $470 billion in treatment, crime, prison construction and upkeep, and other costs. Drugs are the root cause of the scourge of violent crime in the United States—more than one-third of all violent crimes are committed by people hooked on drugs. And drugs are infecting our children's lives at increasing rates, with several recent surveys showing the use of cocaine, marijuana, and hallucinogens increasing in American high schools. The lives, health, and well-being of millions of Americans are thus directly affected by how our government deals with this problem.

The American people and the Colombian people have a common interest in shutting down the drug cartels, and during the past ten years we have sought to cooperate with the Colombian government to do so. To date, the United States has sent $633 million to Colombia in economic and military assistance, including funds to fight the mushrooming drug crisis.

Our policy must be to help the Colombian people fight a real war on drugs. To do so, we must support the efforts of those like Chief Prosecutor Valdivieso, Deputy Chief Prosecutor Adolfo Salamanca, and Colombian National Police chief Jose Serrano, who have brought this narco-corruption to light and are fighting at great personal risk to shut down the cartels. But continued American cooperation with a government led by Mr. Samper—a government in bed with the cartels—would only have postponed the day when a real war on the drug kingpins will be waged.

President Samper, by virtue of his collusion with the cartels, is unfit and unable to lead Colombia in the fight to root this narco-corruption out of the nation's political system. So long as Colombia has a president who is in the pocket of the drug lords, there will be no real crackdown on the cartels.

Mr. Samper should resign. Many in the United States had hoped that Mr. Samper would have the decency to do so and that before the March 1 deadline Colombians would put in place a new government, ready to join with us in a real war on the cartels. Unfortunately, despite the overwhelming evidence against him, President Samper has made clear he will not go quietly and is resisting growing calls within Colombia that he step down. That is his decision, and his future is a decision for the people of Colombia.

But the U.S. government had a decision to make as well. In light of Mr. Samper's collusion with the drug traffickers, America could no longer continue to look the other way. President Clinton was right to decertify Colombia, and as long as Mr. Samper remains in office, there must be no waiver of the law. We look forward to the day when the Colombian people put in place a government that is ready to work together with them and the United States to wage a real war on the drug lords. But letting Mr. Samper and the cartel leaders off the hook again would be in the interest of neither the American people nor the people of Colombia.

DEFEAT THE NARCO-GUERRILLAS
Miami Herald, July 27, 1999

FIVE YEARS AGO, COLOMBIA WAS a pariah state whose then-president, Ernesto Samper, was in bed with the nation's drug barons. Prodded in part by U.S. sanctions, the people threw Samper's party out of office and elected Andres Pastrana. He has taken enormous strides in his first year toward restoring his country's good name.

But Colombia is not out of the woods—not by a long shot. And because Colombia is the source of more than 80 percent of the cocaine flooding America's streets, what happens there is certainly of interest.

Under Samper, the immediate threat to Colombia was narco-corruption within the Colombian government. Today, the threat is from without—from murderous communist guerrillas in league with narco-traffickers. Without U.S. help, Colombia could lose this war. That is why the United States must move swiftly to help President Pastrana.

After taking office, Pastrana attempted to launch a peace process that Colombia's people demanded. The guerrillas answered his call for peace with a relentless campaign of violence. The main guerrilla fronts—the Revolutionary Armed Force of Colombia (FARC) and the National Liberation Army (ELN)—are criminals and terrorists led by a disciplined, ideological cadre (schooled by Fidel Castro) whose aim is to conquer Colombia. They thrive on lawlessness, collecting more than $1 billion annually from drug trafficking, kidnappings, extortion, and ransoms.

These outlaws face a vastly underfunded and outgunned Colombian military. Two-thirds of Colombia's 120,000-man army spends its time and resources protecting bridges, oil pipelines, and power stations. That leaves only 40,000 soldiers, with a mere thirty helicopters, to take on the guerrillas in a rugged, mountainous country almost twice the size of Texas. The 20,000-plus terrorist army, by contrast, wreaks havoc with its hit-and-run tactics.

Despite dramatic—and, quite candidly, questionable—concessions by Pastrana, the guerrillas pay only lip service to the peace process. Since March of this year, a senior FARC commander ordered the cold-blooded murder of three innocent Americans; the ELN has hijacked a Colombian jetliner and committed two mass kidnappings, including one attack on worshipers as they were leaving a church in Cali. On July 8 a five hundred–man terrorist column was intercepted just fifteen miles short of Bogota, Colombia's capital.

What is the United States doing about this growing threat? Very little. At present, virtually all U.S. support to Colombia goes to the antidrug efforts of the Colombian National Police, whose courageous efforts (even under Samper) earned them strong American backing. This is not enough. The U.S. government must exercise bold leadership.

First, it must mobilize international support behind Colombia's new government, its democratic institutions, and the rule of law. There must be no more incidents like the one earlier this year, in which Clinton administration officials held unprecedented meetings with Colombian guerrilla leaders.

Second, we must bolster Colombia's military, beginning with its counterdrug unit, by expanding our training and intelligence assistance, upgrading communications, and increasing their mobility with Blackhawk helicopters. Last year, the Clinton administration fought (unsuccessfully) to stop Congress from giving Blackhawks to Colombian police. Yes, these helicopters are expensive, but the costs of inaction are much higher.

Colombia is one of the most important U.S. trading partners in the Americas, home to $4.5 billion in direct U.S. investment in sectors other than petroleum. The guerrillas have expressly targeted American citizens who live and work in Colombia for kidnappings and murders. Further, the threat to regional stability is acute: Venezuela, Peru, and Ecuador all have massed troops on their borders with Colombia. Panama, which has no army, is helpless to secure its frontier from smugglers of drugs and weapons.

American law requires that any military units receiving U.S. aid must be "scrubbed" for human rights violations, and we must encourage President Pastrana to continue his reforms. However, I am persuaded that increased American support for Colombia's military—which today is slogging through a lonely and desperate struggle with inadequate training and equipment—will in the long run promote human rights.

If America fails to act, Colombia will continue to hurdle toward chaos. If the war drags on—or if desperate Colombians lose their struggle or are forced to appease the narco-guerrillas—the United States and the rest of the hemisphere will pay a price. The longer we delay, the higher that price will be.

Chapter 14
A Compassionate Conservative Foreign Policy

WITH THE ELECTION OF PRESIDENT GEORGE W. BUSH in the fall of 2000, the Clinton era was (finally) coming to a close. Many voices in Washington argued that, with a Senate evenly divided between the parties and a disputed presidential election, Republicans should take a cautious approach.

To the contrary, said Senator Helms. In an address to the American Enterprise Institute just days before the presidential inauguration, Helms declared that, with control not only of the White House but also of both houses of Congress, Republicans must seize this moment of unprecedented opportunity to set the policy agenda in Washington—especially on foreign policy.

Citing President Bush's "compassionate conservative" vision, Senator Helms declared that the wisdom of this philosophy must not stop at the water's edge. He laid out his vision for a "compassionate conservative" foreign policy: revolutionizing the way America delivers foreign assistance by turning to private and faith-based charities closest to those in need; consolidating the last century's democratic advances and continuing the march for freedom in the next; and preserving, protecting, and defending the security and sovereignty of the United States.

TOWARD A COMPASSIONATE
CONSERVATIVE FOREIGN POLICY
An Address to the American Enterprise Institute,
Washington, D.C., January 11, 2001

JOHN BOLTON IS THE KIND OF MAN with whom I would want to stand at Armageddon, if it should be my lot to be on hand for what is forecast to be the final battle between good and evil in this world. John is a great American of courage and wisdom. He loves his country, and I appreciate his coming today to stand with me in my visit with you.

Senator Talmadge used to refer to me as a workhorse—not a show horse. Herman was chairman of the Senate Agriculture Committee when I arrived in Washington in 1973 to become the 1,675th senator to be sworn in since the very first senators took office in 1789.

And just in case you may have some interest in it, let me give you one more statistic: with the swearing-in of those 11 new ones eight days ago, there have now been a total of 1,862 U.S. senators since the birth of the nation. Few of them—and I am one of the few—have not aspired to one day being president.

I am grateful that you invited this (very) old workhorse to be with you today. I shall try to bear in mind that the mind can absorb no more than the seat can endure. And I shall not pretend that I possess magical solutions to all the problems plaguing much of the world today.

The American Enterprise Institute has been around a while, and you have a reputation that many other organizations wish they had. Thank you for inviting me.

In contemplating the arrival of the Bush administration, the several liberal think tanks here in this city are bracing for tough times. Adjusting to life on the sidelines of the public policy debates is not their dish of tea. Eight years of Clinton spoiled them.

On the other hand, few institutions in Washington are more threatened by the Bush inauguration than your American Enterprise Institute. If President Bush does the wise thing, he will raid your treasure trove of brilliant thinkers and appoint all of you to senior positions in his administration. (I hope that he will leave at least a few of you here to continue AEI's important work. Your scholarship is vital to so much of what many of us in Congress try to do.)

You may have noticed that, ever since the November election, the media have been bubbling in hopeful anticipation of my imminent demise. In the past month, I am told, I have been diagnosed with having pancreatic cancer, terminal prostate cancer, and a host of other life-threatening ailments. According to some in the media, I even spent Thanksgiving on a respirator, barely hanging onto life. So your invitation to be with you today enables me to rain on their parade a little.

My purpose in asking John Bolton to gather us together today is obvious, I think. We meet at an important moment in the history of America. As we prepare for the inauguration of the new president, one of the most important tasks America faces is restoring this nation's foreign policy back to the right course.

For six years, I've had the privilege of serving as chairman of the Senate Foreign Relations Committee. And during those six years, Senate Republicans have had some important foreign policy accomplishments of which I hope we can all be proud.

For example, we enacted into law the Libertad (or Helms-Burton) Act, tightening the noose around the neck of the last dictator in the Western Hemisphere—Fidel Castro.

Working with our committee's ranking member, Joe Biden, we took the first steps toward reforming our nation's foreign policy institutions for a post–Cold War world.

We passed historic, bipartisan legislation—the Helms-Biden law—that pays America's so-called UN "arrears" only if there are specific, deep-seated reforms at that dysfunctional institution.

And we passed the National Missile Defense Act, mandating the deployment of missile defenses as soon as the technology is ready.

These are important accomplishments of which we can all be proud. But, as we look back on these successes, it is worth noting that—without exception—every one of these initiatives began either with presidential opposition or the threat of a presidential veto.

Initially, President Clinton vetoed our bipartisan UN reform bill.

The president and his people refused—for almost three years—even to sit down with our committee to discuss our State Department reform proposals.

President Clinton threatened to veto the Libertad Act—he backed down only after Fidel Castro sent Cuban MiG fighters into the Florida Straits to shoot down two unarmed civilian planes (murdering three American citizens in cold blood).

And for eight years, President Clinton did everything in his power to block national missile defense. He changed course only in 1999 after the Rumsfeld Commission delivered its stinging, bipartisan report, leading both houses of Congress to approve missile defense legislation by veto-proof majorities.

The president opposed us on every one of our important initiatives.

And that is just the legislation that we succeeded in forcing through an unwilling White House! The number of important measures that the outgoing Clinton administration succeeded in stopping is simply staggering.

Well, on January 20, all that will change.

On that day we will inaugurate a new president, on whom we can rely to work with us—not against us—in advancing America's interests in the world. And with the appointments of Colin Powell, Condi Rice, and Don Rumsfeld, we will have one of the finest national security teams in the history of this nation. And that will necessarily affect the agenda of the Foreign Relations Committee. Because it expands—dramatically and exponentially—the realm of the possible in terms of what can be accomplished for the American people.

Of course, we will continue to work in a bipartisan manner wherever possible, and I must say that Joe Biden and I have built an excellent working relationship. I believe that the spirit of bipartisan cooperation that Joe and I have established will continue and grow. And while the margin in the Senate has certainly narrowed, let's be honest: Unless either party has sixty votes (enough to invoke cloture and stop debate), then very little can be accomplished in the U.S. Senate without some measure of bipartisan support—no matter who is in control or by how narrow a margin.

But we cannot, and must not, ignore the fact that something has changed in Washington. For the first time in five decades, Republicans will control the White House, the Senate, and the House of Representatives. And that means Republicans can have an unprecedented opportunity to set the policy agenda—especially in the realm of foreign affairs. We must, and we will, seize that opportunity.

And that is why today my purpose is to share with you some of the vital issues on the Foreign Relations Committee's agenda as we prepare for a new administration and the start of the new, 107th Congress.

One of our first priorities come January 20 will be to assist President Bush in implementing his vision of "compassionate conservatism." Now, it might surprise you to find "compassionate conservatism" at the top of the Foreign Relations Committee's agenda; allow me to explain why it's there.

During the fall campaign, President Bush outlined a philosophy of empowering private charities and faith-based institutions to help the neediest of Americans. He declared: "Government can spend money, but it can't put hope in our hearts or a sense of purpose in our lives.... Often when a life is broken, it can only be rebuilt by another caring, concerned human being. Someone whose actions say, 'I love you, I believe in you, I'm in your corner.'"

President Bush continued with this pledge: "In every instance where my administration sees a responsibility to help people, we will look first to faith-based institutions, charities, and community groups that have shown their ability to save and change lives.... We will rally the armies of compassion in our communities to fight a very different war against poverty and hopelessness.... This will not be the failed compassion of towering, distant bureaucracies.... [I]t will be government that [takes] the side of the faith-based organizations and private charities who are helping change lives, one person at a time."

I submit to you, my friends, that the wisdom of this "compassionate conservative" vision must not stop at the water's edge.

During the campaign, President Bush talked about some of the many wonderful faith-based institutions with which he has worked and now admires. One of them is a remarkable organization in my state with which I have been involved—a North Carolina foundation called "Samaritan's Purse."

Samaritan's Purse is led by my longtime friend the Reverend Franklin Graham—the son of a very dear friend, Dr. Billy Graham. I believe that Franklin and his folks at Samaritan's Purse do more good, with less money, for more people around the world than the entire U.S. foreign aid bureaucracy combined.

Want an example? In southern Sudan, where a brutal civil war is tearing a nation apart, Samaritan's Purse runs hospitals and clinics which—despite repeated bombings by government forces—provide desperately needed medical and surgical services to the suffering Sudanese people. Not far from the front lines in the south (in a town called Lui), Samaritan's Purse operates an eighty-bed hospital which has treated more than 100,000 patients—some of whom walk for days across Sudan's plains and swamps to get medical care. More than forty bombs were dropped in March and April last year, and they were bombed again just this week. But the hospital has remained open, and Franklin Graham reports that the brave doctors and nurses there have saved more than 10,000 lives.

Samaritan's Purse has similar projects in more than a hundred countries around the world. In Kosovo, their volunteers have distributed food and medicine, counseled more than three thousand families, and rebuilt at least eight hundred houses. In Central America, after Hurricane Mitch wreaked havoc across the region, they rebuilt more than five thousand homes. And their project "Operation Christmas Child" has distributed more than a million shoe-boxes filled with Christmas toys and gifts to children around the world—in most cases giving these children the first Christmas present they have ever received.

This is incredible work. But Samaritan's Purse is far from alone in this humanitarian endeavor. Their work is complemented every day by the equal efforts of groups such as Catholic Relief Services, World Vision, Save the Children, Hadassa, and many others who are changing lives around the world "one person at a time."

My dear friends, these are the "armies of compassion" that President Bush is talking about. And I put it to you: If we can deploy those "armies of compassion" across America, then we can and must deploy them across the world. The time has come to reject what President Bush correctly labels the "failed compassion of towering, distant bureaucracies" and, instead, empower private and faith-based groups who care most about those in need.

The principle at work here is found in the Christian doctrine of "subsidiarity." Pope John Paul II has put it this way: "Primary responsibility [for helping those in need]...belongs not to the State, but to individuals and to the various groups and associations which make up society.... By intervening directly and depriving society of its responsibility, [government produces]...a loss of human energies and an inordinate increase of public agencies, which are dominated more by bureaucratic ways of thinking than by concern for serving their clients.... [The] needs of the poor are best satisfied by people who were closest to them and who act as neighbors in need."

Not since Ronald Reagan and John Paul II took on Soviet communism have a pope and a president been right on target on such an important issue.

Too often, however, faith-based charities are dismissed by the U.S. foreign aid bureaucracy. The bureaucrats treat them as if the efforts of these faith-based charities are quaint but unworthy of government support. Take, for example, my good friend Father Angelo D'Agostino, a Jesuit priest who runs an orphanage for children suffering from HIV/AIDS in Nuyumbani, Kenya. "Father Dag," as we call him, approached the Agency for International Development for help in supporting his orphanage. AID turned him down. Why? Because, the agency explained, his project did not "fall within USAID's priorities." (You see, since most of the babies he was helping would eventually die of AIDS, his project—by definition—did not meet AID's criteria for "sustainable" development).

I've got news for the AID bureaucrats: What is not sustainable is their cold, heartless, bureaucratic thinking. We must—I repeat, we must—reform the way America helps those in need (not only at home but abroad as well). We must replace the bureaucracy-laden U.S. Agency for International Development with something new.

I intend to work with the Bush administration to replace AID with a new International Development Foundation whose mandate will be to deliver "block grants" to support the work of private relief agencies and faith-based institutions such as Samaritan's Purse, Catholic Relief Services, and countless others like them.

We will reduce the size of America's bloated foreign aid bureaucracy—then take the money saved and use every penny of it to empower these "armies of compassion" to help the world's neediest people.

Those who know me are aware that I have long opposed foreign aid programs that have lined the pockets of corrupt dictators while funding the salaries of a growing, bloated bureaucracy. And I remain adamantly opposed to waste, fraud, and abuse in foreign aid.

But I will make this pledge today: If we can reform the way in which we deliver aid to the needy, based on President Bush's "compassionate conservative" vision—if we can ensure that the taxpayers' money is going to people like Franklin Graham and Father Dag rather than funding a wasteful federal bureaucracy— then I will be willing to take the lead in the Senate in supporting an increased U.S. investment in support of the important endeavors that I have referred to.

While we work to improve the ways America helps those in material need, we must also be attentive to another need—the need for human liberty. Because a foreign policy that does not have freedom at its core is neither compassionate nor conservative.

The 1990s were a decade of enormous democratic advances. In the first years of that decade, we witnessed the collapse of communism in Central and Eastern Europe, and in the final year of the decade, we saw the peaceful transfer of power from long-ruling parties to democratic oppositions in Taiwan and Mexico and the fall of authoritarian leaders in places like Yugoslavia and Peru.

This progress notwithstanding, the global movement toward rule of law, democracy, civil society, and free markets still meets resistance in many quarters. Our challenge in the start of this new millennium—and the start of this new administration—must be to consolidate the democratic advances of the last ten years, while increasing the pressure on those who still refuse to accept the principle that sovereign legitimacy comes from the consent of the governed.

A good place to start is our own hemisphere, and specifically just across our own border. In Mexico, after seventy-one years of one-party rule, the corrupt Institutional Revolutionary Party (or PRI) has finally been voted out of office. President Vicente Fox's victory opens avenues for genuine friendship and cooperation between the United States and Mexico.

President Fox and President Bush already share a constructive vision for dealing with the problems that challenge both of their countries. Working together, we can secure our border, discourage illegal immigration, and strengthen our nation's second-largest trading partner by helping President Fox rejuvenate Mexico's economy. And we can broaden and deepen law enforcement cooperation against the deadly drug trade if both countries attack corruption and impunity.

I will do everything I can to help both presidents set a new course for U.S.-Mexican relations, and I look forward to collaborating with the Bush administration to help set our relationship with the new Mexican government on the right course.

And while democracy has finally taken root across the border in Mexico, just ninety miles from our shores the hemisphere's last totalitarian dictatorship still sputters on. Like a cat with nine lives, Fidel Castro is about to survive his ninth U.S. president. Well, I have a message for Mr. Castro: The last of the cat's nine lives has begun.

Fidel Castro survived the Clinton years for one reason: The Clinton administration never made Castro's removal from power a goal of its foreign policy. Embargo opponents correctly sensed that the Clinton people were never really committed to Castro's isolation and removal, and the administration did nothing to dissuade them of that notion. So they pushed on, dominating the debate. As a result, instead of focusing on developing strategies to undermine Castro and hasten his demise, the last several years in Washington were spent wasting precious time and energy on a senseless debate over whether to lift the Cuban embargo unilaterally.

With the Bush election, the opponents of the Cuban embargo are about to run into a brick wall on the other end of Pennsylvania Avenue. President Bush is a committed supporter of the embargo. Cuban-Americans recognized the real thing when they saw it, and they turned out in record numbers to support him in Florida— giving Mr. Bush the margin that secured Florida's twenty-five electoral votes and the White House.

What this means is that, with the embargo finally off the table, the new Bush administration has a golden opportunity to develop a new Cuba policy. The model for such a new Cuba policy should be the successful policies that the Reagan-Bush administration used in the 1980s to undermine communism in Poland.

In the 1980s, the U.S. hastened Poland's democratic transformation by isolating the communist regime in Warsaw while at the same time actively lifting the isolation of the Polish people—supporting the democratic opposition and cultivating an emerging civil society with financial and other means of support.

We must now do the same thing in Cuba. In 1998, I introduced legislation—the Cuban Solidarity Act—which proposed, among other measures, giving $100 million in U.S. government humanitarian aid to the Cuban people (to be delivered not through the Cuban government but through private charitable institutions functioning on the island). Such private assistance will help give Cubans independence from the state, which now controls their lives by controlling their access to food, medicine, and other daily necessities.

Come January 20, I intend to work with the Bush administration to do for the people of Cuba what the United States did for the people of Poland twenty years ago. And I will make a prediction here today: Before his term is up, President Bush will visit Havana—to attend the inauguration of the new democratically elected president of Cuba.

Another place where democracy desperately needs renewed American support is in Taiwan. A remarkable thing happened in Taiwan at the close of the twentieth century. With the election of President Chen last year, the people of Taiwan presided over the first peaceful transfer of power from a ruling party to its democratic opposition in five thousand years of Chinese history.

This was an incredible achievement—and an ultimate repudiation of the myth spread by Beijing's dictators and their allies that Western democracy is incompatible with so-called "Asian values." How sad, therefore, that while Taiwan was undertaking these incredible democratic advances, the Clinton policy of deliberately eroding U.S. support for Taiwan did enormous damage.

President Clinton repeatedly let down our friends in Taiwan, first by going to China and repeating Beijing's fictitious constructions on the future of Taiwan and then by refusing to meet America's legal obligations to provide for Taiwan's self-defense under the Taiwan Relations Act.

This damage must be undone. The military balance of power of the past twenty years is quickly shifting in Beijing's favor. Because of the Clinton administration's neglect, Taiwan's self-defense capabilities are not keeping up with Beijing's rapid military modernization. It is imperative that we act quickly to reverse the decline.

Yes, we must engage China. But Beijing also must be made to understand that its avenues to destructive behavior are closed off and that Taiwan will have the means to defend itself. During the campaign, President Bush gave his enthusiastic endorsement to the Taiwan Security Enhancement Act (TSEA). And I intend to work with him to enact the TSEA and to help ensure that Taiwan's democracy remains secure from Chinese aggression.

Another place where aggression is being rewarded because of the Clinton administration's neglect is Iraq. For the last eight years, we have watched as the Clinton administration has presided over the collapse of our Iraq policy. The Clinton people have abandoned weapons inspections, abandoned sanctions, and, ultimately, abandoned the people of Iraq themselves.

We must have a new Iraq policy, and such a policy must be based on a clear understanding of this salient fact: Nothing will change in Iraq until Saddam Hussein is removed from power. Almost a decade has gone by since the United States liberated Kuwait from Saddam Hussein. The time has come to liberate Iraq as well. With the passage of the bipartisan Iraq Liberation Act, Congress took the lead in promoting the democratic opposition to Saddam Hussein. (The Clinton administration failed to implement the act.) I look forward to working with President Bush to implement effectively the Iraq Liberation Act to help the people of Iraq get rid of Saddam Hussein.

Perhaps the greatest moral challenge we face at the dawn of a new century is to right the wrongs perpetrated in the last century at Yalta, when the West abandoned the nations of Central and Eastern Europe to Stalin and a life of servitude behind the Iron Curtain.

We began the process of righting that wrong in 1998, when the Senate voted to admit Poland, Hungary, and the Czech Republic into the NATO alliance. I consider it one of my proudest moments as chairman of the Senate Foreign Relations Committee to have helped usher in those three nations' admission to NATO and thus to have helped them secure their rightful place in the community of Western democracies.

But the admission of Poland, Hungary, and the Czech Republic has not yet fully erased the scars of Yalta. During the Cold War, I was one of a group of senators who fought to defend the independence of what came to be known as the "Captive Nations" (the Baltic states of Lithuania, Latvia, and Estonia)— and who worked to make sure that the United States never recognized their illegal annexation by the Soviet Union.

With the collapse of communism, those nations finally achieved their rightful independence from Russian occupation and domination. Yet Russia still looms menacingly over these countries. In looking at the current Russian government, one gets the distinct impression that the Russian leadership considers Baltic independence to be a temporary phenomenon. That is an impression that the Russians cannot be allowed to long entertain.

Just as we never recognized the Soviet annexation of the Baltic states, we must not repeat the mistakes of the 1940s today by acknowledging a Russian sphere of influence in what Russian leaders ominously call the "near abroad." These nations' independence will never be fully secure until they are safe from the threat of Russian domination and are fully integrated into the community of Western democracies.

I intend to work with the Bush administration to ensure that the Baltic states are invited to join their neighbors Poland, Hungary, and the Czech Republic as members of the NATO alliance. This is vital not only for their security but for ours as well. If we want good relations with Russia, we must show Russia's leaders an open path to good relations, while at the same time closing off their avenues to destructive behavior. That means taking the next step in the process of NATO expansion, by issuing invitations to the Baltic nations when NATO's leaders meet for the next alliance summit planned for 2002.

Another immediate priority is national missile defense. After eight lost years under President Clinton, we have no time to waste in building and deploying a truly national missile defense that is capable of protecting the United States and its allies from ballistic missile attack.

Last year, when President Clinton threatened to negotiate a revised ABM Treaty with Russia that would tie the hands of the new administration, I went to the Senate floor and warned Mr. Clinton that any such agreement would be dead on arrival in the U.S. Senate.

Now, as President Bush prepares to take office, I want to make something perfectly clear to our friends in Russia. The United States is no longer bound by the ABM Treaty—that treaty expired when our treaty partner (the Soviet Union) ceased to exist. Legally speaking, the Bush administration faces no impediment whatsoever to proceeding with any national missile defense system it chooses to deploy.

President Bush may decide that it is in the United States' diplomatic interests to sit down with the Russians and discuss his plans for missile defense. Personally, I do not think that a new ABM Treaty can be negotiated with Russia that would permit the kind of defenses America needs. But, as Henry Kissinger told the Foreign Relations Committee last year, "I would be open to argument, provided that we do not use the treaty as a constraint on pushing forward on the most effective development of a national and theater missile defense."

With that caveat by Dr. Kissinger, I concur—President Bush must have, and will have, the freedom to proceed as he sees fit. And I look forward to working with the president to ensure that he achieves his goal of a rapid deployment of an effective and truly national missile defense.

Last but not least, ladies and gentlemen, there is the issue of the International Criminal Court.

Let me be perfectly clear: All of the issues I have discussed today are of immense importance. But if I do nothing else this year, I will make certain that President Clinton's outrageous and unconscionable decision to sign the Rome treaty establishing the International Criminal Court is reversed and repealed.

Two years ago, President Clinton refused to sign the Rome treaty. The reason for his refusal, as Mr. Clinton's chief negotiator, Ambassador David Scheffer, told Congress at the time, was simple. "The [Rome] treaty," Ambassador Scheffer declared, "purports to establish an arrangement whereby United States armed forces operating overseas could be conceivably prosecuted by the International Criminal Court even if the United States has not agreed to be bound by the treaty. Not only is this contrary to the most fundamental principles of treaty law, it could inhibit the ability of the United States to use its military to meet alliance obligations and participate in multinational operations."

Nothing—I repeat, nothing—has changed since Ambassador Scheffer uttered those words to justify the president's signature. The court still claims today, as it did two years ago, to hold the power to indict, try, and imprison American citizens—even if the American people refuse to join the court.

This brazen assault on the sovereignty of the American people is without precedent in the annals of international treaty law.

There are two things I will press for with the new administration. First, the Bush administration should simply un-sign the Rome statute. I mean, quite literally, that the administration should instruct someone at the U.S. Mission in New York to walk across the street to the UN, ask to see the treaty document, and then take out a pen and draw a line through Ambassador Scheffer's name. I think that will send a clear message.

Second, we must enact the American Servicemembers Protection Act. This legislation, which Senator Warner and I introduced last year along with a number of our House and Senate colleagues, is designed to protect U.S. citizens from the jurisdiction of the International Criminal Court.

Our effort was publicly endorsed last month by a bipartisan group of former senior U.S. officials, including (among others) President Bush's defense secretary–designate, Don Rumsfeld, Henry Kissinger, George Shultz, James Baker, Brent Scowcroft, Jeane Kirkpatrick, Caspar Weinberger, and Jim Woolsey.

Why is passage of this legislation important? Because by signing this flawed treaty, President Clinton has effectively endorsed the ICC's fraudulent claim of jurisdiction over Americans. We must take action to make clear that, unless and until the United States ratifies the Rome treaty, we reject any claim of jurisdiction by the ICC over American citizens. Period.

The nations pushing this court on the American people may have thought that they could push, cajole, and triangulate the self-proclaimed "Man from Hope." Well, they need to understand that, come January 20, there is a new president in town with a new motto they had better learn: "Don't mess with Texas."

These, ladies and gentlemen, are my priorities. As you can see, the Foreign Relations Committee will have a full agenda in the coming year. From revolutionizing the way America delivers foreign assistance; to consolidating the last century's democratic advances and continuing the march for freedom in the next; to preserving, protecting, and defending the security and sovereignty of the United States—we will have our work cut out for us as we seek to restore a foreign policy that is both compassionate and conservative.

And to accomplish these tasks, we will need your invaluable assistance. As I said at the outset, AEI is one of the most exceptional institutions in Washington. I am enormously proud of the work you do and honored that you've taken time from your busy schedules to be with me this afternoon.

I hope that we can count on your help in the coming year to make this ambitious agenda a reality. And—whether as AEI scholars or representatives of the Bush administration—I look forward to seeing many of you at the witness table of the Senate Foreign Relations Committee in the months ahead.

Thank you for your patience—and your thoughtful invitation for me to be with you today.

Chapter 15

The Reagan Revolution and a Moral Foreign Policy

IN MARCH OF 2001, THE U.S. NAVY christened a new aircraft carrier—the USS *Ronald Reagan.*

To celebrate the occasion, the Reagan Presidential Foundation asked Senator Helms to speak on President Reagan's enduring legacy. In his remarks, given at a Washington luncheon, Senator Helms recalled Ronald Reagan's upset victory over Gerald Ford in the 1976 North Carolina primary—an event that revitalized his flagging campaign and made possible his 1980 run for the White House (and thus the Reagan presidency).

The 1976 campaign was a turning point not just in Ronald Reagan's career, Helms said, but in American foreign policy as well.

Coming into North Carolina, Reagan had lost five consecutive primaries to Ford. Everyone was saying he was finished. Reagan turned the race around by making foreign policy—specifically, the Ford-Kissinger policy of détente with the Soviet Union—the central issue of his campaign.

The American people sensed that we were losing the Cold War, Senator Helms said. Reagan criticized détente, making the case that America should stop being afraid of standing up for freedom and shouldn't seek "peaceful coexistence" with Soviet tyranny. America's battle with Soviet communism, he said, was not simply a struggle for a better "balance of power"; it was a battle between right and wrong, between good and evil. He called for a moral foreign policy.

Kissinger complained that Reagan was "trigger-happy" and "inciting hawkish audiences with his demagoguery." But Americans started responding to Ronald Reagan's vision of a moral foreign policy.

It would be more than four years before Reagan took the oath of office as the fortieth president of the United States and began implementing his moral vision of American foreign policy. But the 1976 campaign was a turning point.

And, Senator Helms declared, the effects of that seismic shift Ronald Reagan brought to American foreign policy are still being felt a decade after Reagan left office: "The Reagan agenda is still our agenda today: principled American leadership on the world stage; a commitment to freedom under God as the organizing bedrock of our foreign policy; unmatched military might and concrete defenses for the American people; limited government and growth-oriented tax cuts that keep our prosperity going; and a commitment to give every one of our citizens a shot at the American dream."

In this speech, Senator Helms discusses the origins of a dramatic shift in American politics and American foreign policy—a shift that "not only won Ronald Reagan the North Carolina primary, it also won the Cold War."

<hr>

THE LASTING LEADERSHIP OF RONALD REAGAN
A Speech Celebrating the Christening of the
USS *Ronald Reagan*, Washington, D.C., March 2, 2001

MY FIRST MEETING WITH RONALD REAGAN seemed pleasant but unremarkable. It took place in the early 1960s, when I was executive vice president of a television station in Raleigh (some time earlier, WRAL had become the second TV station in the country to begin televised editorials). When that smiling, soft-spoken, likable, youngish gentleman stopped by WRAL, I instantly recognized him as "the movie star."

We talked about Hollywood, and the media, and editorializing, and—of course—politics. He knew that I had worked for a while in Washington for a conservative senator from North Carolina who died after less than three years in office.

He suggested at the outset of the conversation that I call him "Ron," not "Mr. Reagan." We agreed to first-name each other—and, out of the blue, with that inimitable smile and those twinkling eyes, he asked, "Are you going to run for office someday?"

I said no—but that I sure hoped he would.

He hesitated a moment, then said, "I'm thinking about it."

Well, thank the Lord he did more than think about it. Ron Reagan did run for public office soon thereafter. In 1966 he was elected governor of California. We kept in touch. And, in 1972, when I ran for the U.S. Senate (convinced that I would not be elected), he supported me and even did a TV ad for my campaign.

So there we were, a widely known governor of California and I, the first Republican ever elected to the United States Senate by the people of North Carolina. The liberal media had already been criticizing Governor Reagan for being "too conservative" and saying he'd be a one-termer because he was "just an actor." Now they were chuckling about how I would be a one-term senator because I was one of those right-wing nuts.

Then came the Nixon disaster and Gerald Ford's being elevated from appointed vice president to the presidency—and his subsequent candidacy for election to the presidency.

Ronald Reagan ran against Ford in that race. Now, taking on a sitting president of one's own party is no easy task. But Ronald Reagan gave it his best shot. Yet in that 1976 campaign, Ron was in rough shape coming into the North Carolina primary, having lost five consecutive primaries to President Ford. The people were saying he was finished; the Ford people cranked up the pressure for Ron to get out of the race; nine of his fellow Republican governors issued a statement calling on Ron to withdraw; even some of his own advisors were telling him to throw in the towel.

But Ronald Reagan wouldn't give up—and if he wasn't giving up, we weren't about to give up on him. Tom Ellis and the folks at the Congressional Club went all out for Ron, putting together a travel schedule across North Carolina for him and Nancy. Dot and I campaigned with him: Nancy and Dot went east; Ron and I went west. Jimmy Stewart came to North Carolina and barnstormed the state for his friend.

Sam Donaldson was among the Washington reporters there covering the race in North Carolina. At just about every campaign stop, Sam would bellow, "Governor, Governor Reagan! When are you getting out?" And (in a ritual that would later become familiar to the American people) Ron Reagan would smile, cup his hand to his ear, pretending he couldn't make out what Sam was saying, and keep on walking.

In any event, Ronald Reagan campaigned his heart out, but he left North Carolina absolutely convinced he was going to lose. He didn't lose. He carried North Carolina, 52 percent to 46 percent. It was the first time in a quarter century that a sitting president had been defeated in a primary. And a few weeks later, Ron went on to Texas—and won again. The Reagan campaign was on a roll, and suddenly we had a real race on our hands.

What turned the tide in 1976? The answer is simple: Ronald Reagan campaigned on principles. He made clear where he stood—and North Carolina stood with him.

Prior to his North Carolina victory, a lot of self-appointed experts had been warning Ron to tone down his conservatism to make himself appear more "mainstream" and thereby acceptable to middle America. That strategy lost him five states in a row, and by the North Carolina primary, thank the Lord, the time had come to let Reagan be Reagan.

Ron Reagan took on the Ford-Kissinger policy of détente with the Soviet Union. Ron sensed that the American people felt we were losing the Cold War. They saw that country after country was falling to communism, American resolve was faltering, and the Soviets were pulling ahead of us in the race for military superiority.

Ronald Reagan made his case to the American people that we should stand up for freedom instead of seeking "peaceful coexistence" with Soviet tyranny. He called for rebuilding America's defense capabilities. He declared that "peace does not come from weakness or retreat—it comes from the restoration of American military superiority."

He condemned immoral agreements such as the Helsinki accord, in which, he said, the Ford administration had put "America's stamp of approval on Russia's enslavement of the captive nations ... [and had given] away the freedom of millions of people—freedom that was not ours to give." He called for an end to "balance of power" diplomacy and declared that our battle with Soviet communism was not simply a struggle between rival powers but rather a battle between right and wrong, between good and evil.

Henry Kissinger declared that Ron was "trigger-happy" and said that Ron was "inciting hawkish audiences with his demagoguery." But the American people began responding.

At the GOP convention in Kansas City, Reagan fought to include a "Morality in Foreign Policy" plank in the Republican platform. At his insistence (and over the objections of the Ford forces), the GOP platform that year declared that, henceforth, "the goal of Republican foreign policy is the achievement of liberty under law and a just and lasting peace in the world." The platform declared forthrightly that "we must face the world with no illusions about the nature of tyranny" and that the United States must not conclude agreements with the Soviets that "take away from those who do not have freedom the hope of one day gaining it" (a direct repudiation of the Helsinki accord). And it concluded, "Honestly, openly, and with a firm conviction, we shall go forward as a united people to forge a lasting peace in the world based on our deep belief in the rights of man, the rule of law, and guidance by the hand of God."

It was a thrilling turning point in American history. Of course, Ronald Reagan didn't win the nomination that year. But his strong showing staked his claim as the front-runner for the nomination in 1980—and laid down a marker that the days of coddling Soviet tyranny were coming to an end.

Ronald Reagan's willingness to stand up for a foreign policy based on principle not only won him the North Carolina primary, it also won the Cold War.

Success, it is said, has many fathers. And America's victory in the Cold War has innumerable claims of paternity. It did not take long after the fall of the Berlin Wall before everyone in Washington began claiming to have been "on the right side" of the battle for freedom and that back then "we all agreed" on the need to confront and defeat Soviet communism.

Hogwash. Things were not "easy" during the Cold War, and we did not "all agree." The liberals howled when Ronald Reagan declared the Soviet Union an "Evil Empire." Their blood curdled when he declared his intention to leave communism on the "ash heap of history." They opposed his efforts to build SDI; they opposed his effort to rebuild our nation's military; they opposed his efforts to support freedom fighters seeking to overthrow communist regimes in our hemisphere and around the world. They fought him every step of the way.

As always, President Reagan himself put it best. In 1992, when he addressed the Republican National Convention for the last time, he said: "I heard those speakers at that other convention saying, 'We won the Cold War.' And I couldn't help wondering... just who exactly do they mean by 'we'?"

Ronald Reagan won the Cold War! But his victory in the Cold War was only the first of many instances in which his opponents sought to associate themselves with his successes and co-opt his ideas.

I don't think it's possible to overstate just how deeply President Reagan affected—and continues to affect—the American political landscape. The Reagan presidency was an event of seismic proportions—a shift in the tectonic plates of American politics.

Ronald Reagan, it has been said, made the Clinton presidency possible. This is not to besmirch the reputation of our good friend President Reagan but rather to demonstrate just how fundamentally Ronald Reagan's ideas altered the ground rules of American politics.

When Bill Clinton took office in 1992, his and Hillary's very first project was their effort to nationalize American health care. It was an old-style, left-wing, big government project—and it was a colossal failure. The American people wanted nothing to do with a return to big government liberalism. And to make sure Mr. Clinton got the message, they went to the polls in 1994, turned out the Democrat Congress, and elected a Republican majority— a stinging, personal repudiation of Bill Clinton.

Bill Clinton got the message. By 1996 he was standing before a Republican Congress declaring, "We know big government does not have all the answers. We know there is not a program for every problem.... The era of big government is over."

With that one statement, Bill Clinton was conceding Ronald Reagan's victory in the war of ideas. With that statement, Clinton acknowledged that, thanks to the Reagan Revolution, a

Democratic president could no longer govern the nation on the basis of the Democratic orthodoxy of big government liberalism. That orthodoxy had been repudiated by Ronald Reagan and rejected by the American people. And the only way a Democratic president could govern and expect to be reelected was to do his best to imitate Ronald Reagan.

Needless to say, Bill Clinton was no Ronald Reagan—never was and never will be. Indeed, it was against the backdrop of the dignity Ronald Reagan brought to the presidency that Bill Clinton's moral failures were so shamefully exposed. Ronald Reagan would not take his jacket off in the Oval Office; Bill Clinton could not keep his trousers on.

But Clinton did his best to steal pages from the Reagan playbook. And when the history books mention the Clinton years—after the entries on Monica Lewinsky and Marc Rich—they may note that Clinton ran a couple of successful plays from the Gipper's game plan. They will note the expansion of North American free trade to Mexico, the passage of welfare reform, the expansion of the NATO alliance to include the former "captive nations" of the Warsaw Pact. And, if they are honest, they will note that each and every one of these accomplishments was lifted from the agenda of Ronald Wilson Reagan.

Publicly, Clinton tried calling his approach the "Third Way." Privately, the term was "triangulation." But whatever he chose to call it, it was nothing more than a smokescreen behind which a Democratic president sought to hide the fact that he was stealing ideas from Ronald Reagan.

Today we have (finally) returned to the true way forged by Ronald Reagan. We have a new president we can be proud of—a president who is not ashamed to embrace the enduring legacy of President Reagan.

In his speech at the Reagan Library in 1999, then-governor Bush declared, "We live in the nation President Reagan restored, and the world he helped to save." It was an appropriate venue, for so much of what President Bush is seeking to accomplish for America is the continuation of the Reagan Revolution—and the completion of its unfinished agenda.

At the Reagan Library, Bush rejected isolationism as a "short-cut to chaos,... an approach that abandons our allies, and our ideals... [whose] result, in the long run, would be a stagnant America and a savage world." Many in the media reported this as a tactical shift to the center—an effort to distance himself from the conservative wing of the party. Nothing could be further from the truth.

In point of fact, Bush was calling on Americans to heed the call of Ronald Reagan, who exhorted us in his farewell address at the Houston convention to reject "the new isolationists [who] claim the American people don't care about how or why we prevailed in the great defining struggle of our age... [and] who insist that our triumph is yesterday's news, part of a past that holds no lessons for the future."

But the consensus for vigorous, "distinctly American" leadership on the world stage is only the beginning of the legacy Ronald Reagan left us. Consider just some of the things we take for granted in American political life today that would never have happened were it not for the leadership of President Reagan.

For example: missile defense. In 1983, when Ronald Reagan declared America's intention to build and deploy strategic missile defenses, liberals ridiculed it as science fiction—"Star Wars," they called it. That was then. In 1999, after eight wasted years under Bill Clinton, Congress passed the National Missile Defense Act, mandating the deployment of missile defenses—and did so by a bipartisan, veto-proof majority. There is today a consensus in Washington on the need for a defense to protect the American people from ballistic missile attack, and President Bush has declared building and deploying missile defenses his single most important national security priority.

Or take the economy. When Ronald Reagan argued twenty years ago that the way to get the economy moving again was to cut taxes to spur economic growth, the left howled its rage. The liberal media sought to make "Reaganomics" a bad word. That was then. Today, after two decades of the virtually uninterrupted economic expansion that Ronald Reagan set in motion, the economy is slowing down—and everyone in Washington agrees that a tax cut is needed to spur economic growth.

Think about it: The Democrats want to cut taxes by $900 billion, the Republicans want to cut taxes by $1.6 trillion, and we will fight over the numbers. But there is consensus in Washington on the need for tax cuts, and no one in the political mainstream today contests the principle that cutting marginal rates is the key to economic growth. That is the legacy of Ronald Reagan at work.

Or how about "compassionate conservatism"? I suggest that Ronald Reagan was the original "compassionate conservative." Listen to the commission President Reagan gave the Republican Party and the American people in Houston nine years ago, in his farewell address, when he called for conservatives to declare war on poverty the same way we declared war on Soviet communism. "Just as we have led the crusade for democracy beyond our shores, we have a great task to do together in our own home," President Reagan told us. "With each sunrise we are reminded that millions of our citizens have yet to share in the abundance of American prosperity. Many languish in neighborhoods riddled with drugs and bereft of hope. Still others hesitate to venture out onto the streets for fear of criminal violence. Let us pledge ourselves to a new beginning for them."

How do we do that? Start with education, President Reagan told us: "Let us apply our ingenuity and remarkable spirit to revolutionize education in America, so that every one of us will have the mental skills to build a better life." (Or, as President Bush has put it, let's make certain that "no child is left behind.")

Next, President Reagan told us, we must make sure that the engine of economic growth touches every American community. "Let us harness the competitive energy that built America into rebuilding our inner cities," President Reagan said, "so that real jobs can be created for those who live there and real hope can rise out of despair." (Or, as President Bush has put it, we must have "prosperity with a purpose.")

And let us never forget, President Reagan declared, that the American dream must be open to every American: "Whether we are Afro-American or Irish-American; Christian or Jewish; from big cities or small towns, we are equal in the eyes of God.... In America our origins matter less than our destinations, and that is what democracy is all about."

A decade after he left office, the Reagan agenda is still our agenda today: principled American leadership on the world stage; a commitment to freedom under God as the organizing bedrock of our foreign policy; unmatched military might and concrete defenses for the American people; limited government and growth-oriented tax cuts that keep our prosperity going; and a commitment to give every one of our citizens a shot at the American dream.

Ronald Reagan's voice may have been silenced by Alzheimer's disease, but his vision and his principled leadership will forever continue speak to our future.

Before he left us for that journey leading him "into the sunset of [his] life," President Reagan laid out a parting vision for the Republican Party and the conservative movement. It is a vision that I believe is shared, in the most heartfelt way, by our new president, George W. Bush. In President Bush we have a leader worthy of the mantle of Ronald Reagan—a leader who will not only continue the Reagan Revolution but also take that revolution, shape it, build it, and move it forward in his own unique way. I know Ronald Reagan would be proud of him—and would be pleased to see a man so worthy of the office once again sitting at his desk.

And while we honor President Reagan, let us remember that we are not merely commemorating past glories. Rather, we are renewing our commitment to a living revolution, an ongoing and unfinished agenda, and the lasting leadership of Ronald Reagan.

Permissions

defense, to reform of the United Nations, to the situation in the Middle East, to expansion of NATO—he shows how the United States must proceed in the post–Cold War world. Indeed, he demonstrates how contemporary calls for "multilateralism" undermine the very international order that won the Cold War.

Finally, Senator Helms lays out his vision for how America can proceed with a "compassionate conservative" foreign policy under President George W. Bush—that is, how President Bush's compassionate conservatism must not stop at the water's edge.